KNOW YOUR FINANCIAL RIGHTS

BATTLE MANUALS FOR FREEDOM
BOOK 3

A. LE ROY

UNPARAGONED

Formatted with Vellum

BATTLE MANUALS FOR FREEDOM

GENI.US/RIGHTS

Book 1: *Know Your Medical Rights*

Book 2: *Know Your Lawful Rights*

Book 3: *Know Your Financial Rights*

Book 4: *Know Your Spiritual Rights*

CONTENTS

INTRODUCTION

And each in the cell of himself is almost convinced of his freedom.

— W.H. AUDEN, *IN MEMORY OF W.B. YEATS*

WE HAVE BEEN HORRIBLY RIPPED OFF!

In your heart, you know this. From dawn to dusk, from cradle to grave, we have been tax-farmed, fined, and fleeced. We have been stripped of our dignity, prodded, probed, and poked, and ordered about by half-wits who have not one shred of courage, integrity, or truth in their hearts. Brothers and Sisters, I have had enough, and this *Battle Manual for Freedom* is my response.

I wrote *Know Your Medical Rights* (originally titled *The COVID Protocols: Upholding Your Rights in Authoritarian Times*) as a weapon against the medical tyranny that, starting in 2020, sought to desecrate our constitutional protections. Job done, or so I thought.

But as we now know, COVID was just the opening assault. We are also being assailed by poisons in our food, water, earth, and air; engineered shortages, and sabotage; radiation and energy weapons; along with war, assassination programs, fabricated emergencies, and false-flag terrorism.

Among other forms of attack are: lawless legislation and destructive regulation; impositions of a counterfeit righteousness; censorship, propaganda, fear-mongering, and indoctrination; monitoring and surveillance; digital imprisonment and technocracy; demoralization and destruction of hope; separation, isolation, and division; demolition of the family, culture, and meritocracy; stolen elections; weaponized immigration; ecological devastation and pollution (nothing to do with carbon-dioxide, by the way); and overall treason by politicians, bureaucrats, agencies, corporations, courts, and police.

To counter all this, I wrote the next book, *Know Your Lawful Rights,* but even then, the work was not finished, for the predator class are coming at us with all manner of financial attack too, including murderous levels of taxation, inflation, debt, and confiscation of assets and property. Meanwhile, bank runs, bank failures, and bank freezes are looming, and even bank bail-ins, where they just help themselves to the contents of your account.

On the other side of this obliteration, our enemies plan central-bank digital currencies (CBDC), where they can reward your behaviour if they like it, and penalize your behaviour and speech if they don't, and make further deductions on a whim without giving you recourse. Hence this third and final book in the series, *Know Your Financial Rights*.

I recall the horrifying scenes of pallets of cash left behind when the U.S. military bolted from Afghanistan in 2021. However worthless, that paper represents the toil of millions of Americans whose life's work has been squandered by a vampiric cabal hell-bent on enriching themselves while destroying us.

We know in our hearts we were not put on this Earth to supply these parasites. We who are in Christ also remember that his yoke is easy and his burden is light (*Matthew* 11:28-30). Like the kin of Moses longing to break free from Egypt and its state-sanctioned death cult, we too long for our Exodus and restoration of our Birthright. May this book sever the chains that held us, especially the spiritual ones, for if our minds are free, our reality shall follow. This requires us to dispel the delusions and mind-tricks that have been played on us for centuries, even millennia.

When it comes to solutions, I do not claim to be the tip of the spear; others have done more battle than I. Rather, my contribution is to bring into coherence the myriad fragments of wisdom, analysis, and experience that are out there, and above all to clarify them. As I said, Christ's burden is light, and that includes the financial one. If solutions are too complicated for the layman to grasp, I will simplify them if possible and discard them if not.

Nor am I am setting out to prescribe one-size-fits-all remedies. "There is no magic bullet," to quote Si 'the Spaniard' of youandyourcash.com, when I attended one of his seminars in England. "You're the magic bullet." You will pick and choose from the tools at your disposal and play to your particular strengths.

That is our key advantage as we undermine, obstruct, and overthrow the evil plans of financial despots. Wise as serpents, we are inventing strategies and approaches so numerous and varied that the enemy cannot possibly find an answer to all of them. Compared to the one-government, one-narrative, one-opinion, one-way, one-rule, one-religion, one-food, one-health, one-medicine, and one-currency brigade opposing us, we are a motley crew, but I celebrate that. As C.S. Lewis wrote, "Good, as it ripens, becomes continually more different, not only from evil, but from other good."1

Now, as you may be aware, I just quoted Scripture with "wise as serpents" (*Matthew* 10:16). Some readers have complained that I speak too much of spiritual battle in this book series and about the victory of Christ and his prophets over Satan's schemes and schemers.

To which I say, deal with it. If you think you're going to get through the battles ahead against foes who are themselves deeply religious and who are supernaturally allied with infernal forces, then you will be easy meat for their murderous agenda. Also, if my offering is good fruit from a holy root, it were blasphemous to reject the tree that produced it.

Jesus—or Yeshua or Yehusha if you prefer—gave us

authority to overcome all the power of the enemy (*Luke* 10:19). In addition to this spiritual authority, we have the authority of logic because, as the documentary *Strawman* reminds us, "Government is a creation of man, and a creation of man can never be above man."

This authority equates to that of the Lawful realm, meaning that which the Most High bestows, over the Legal realm, which is what men write, revise, and repeal. Which raises the question: Why bother operating in the Legal arena at all—with its politicians, bureaucrats, autocrats, and technocrats, its corporations and courts, so-called lawyers and police? Only because they have a nasty habit of showing up where they're not wanted and not needed. We are to put them back in their inferior places and disabuse them of their power-hungry ambitions to play God in the lives of others.

As Shakespeare observed, "All the world's a stage/ And all the men and women merely players" (*As You Like It*, II.vii.). Sometimes, we are called to put on a costume and play a role in the Theatre of the Legal, but we are not *of* the Legal. When the play is over, we take off the costume, resume our higher life, and leave behind those who are trapped in the Legal illusion and think it is real and all that there is.

Much love,
Abdiel LeRoy

1

TAXATION IS DEAD TO US

Tyrants would distribute largess, a bushel of wheat, a gallon of wine, and a sesterce, and then everybody would shamelessly cry, "Long live the King!" The fools did not realize that they were merely recovering a portion of their own property, and that their ruler could not have given them what they were receiving without having first taken it from them…

— ÉTIENNE DE LA BOETIE,
THE POLITICS OF OBEDIENCE, 1553

It makes no sense when you think about it. Birds get to build their nests and feed their young from the resources around them. They are not required to give a portion of their labour to other birds. Same goes for the squirrel of the tree or the fish of the sea. But not so for us. We men and women are fined just for daring to live and breathe on this Earth.

"Why do we have to pay to live on a planet we were born on?" asks Jeff Harry in a TikTok video recorded in 2022. "And who are we actually paying for the privilege of being alive here? Who made them the boss? Who put them in charge?"

I'll qualify my statement about the birds, though. Sometimes a cuckoo will come along and lay an egg in the nest of another bird. After hatching, the baby cuckoo will evict the rightful inheritors of the nest and fool the parent into feeding it instead. In that case, the animal kingdom *does* represent the trick the predator class play on us through taxation. As David E. Robinson writes in *Meet Your Strawman*,...

> "It has long since reached a ridiculous level, with the average person being expected to pay Income Tax, Council Tax, Inheritance Tax, National Insurance, Capital Gains Tax, Sales Tax on house purchases, Value Added Tax, Parking charges, Airport charges, Fuel Tax, Road Tax, Import Duty, Tax on alcohol, Tax on tobacco, payments for a driving licence, passport... the list goes on and on and on with additional items added all the time."

Suppose I want to join a club. I apply for membership, pay a fee, and agree to the club rules. But what if some club I never joined decided to charge me a membership fee anyway, insisted I obey its rules, and made secret decisions that caused harm to me or my loved ones? I'd be livid. So would you. Yet that is exactly how governments behave. I never signed up to be bullied or extorted, and neither did you.

The Status of Man

How, then, shall we be liberated? First, by renewing our minds. As author Larken Rose laments in a splendid rant recorded in 2024,...

> "When that tiny group of parasites says, 'You have to give us a ton of money every year,' the throng doesn't say, 'No, we don't!' It says, 'We really wish you would tell us that we're allowed to not quite give you as much money as we did last year... Oh, we love the master that lets us keep more of what we produce.' "

If that's your mindset, Rose continues, "You're already 100% a slave in your own mind when all you can comprehend is begging the master to let you keep some more of what you produce."

In *Know Your Lawful Rights,* I describe how governments, which are corporations, assert false jurisdiction over us by levying taxes, fines, and fees against a corporate fiction—the 'STRAWMAN'—using a fake version of Our Names spelled in ALL CAPS. They want to flatten us from the living, breathing, three-dimensional beings that we are into a two-dimensional page, for their corporate fictions can only interact with other corporate fictions, much as characters in a play interact with other characters in that play.

I also looked at the Birth Certificate, and how the banking cabal use it to trade our lifetime's labour, creativity, and time. The three-dimensional Truth, however, is that we remain in authority over the fictions of men.

I considered too what it means to have 'Dominion' of the Earth (*Genesis* 1:26-28), that this would bestow on each of us productive land four times the size of Twickenham rugby field. (That's if the Earth is as small as they tell us it is.) Therefore, on your behalf and mine, dear Reader, let us stand together now before the throne of the Most High and claim in Heaven our portion of the Earth, knowing that when we agree on this, it is done for us by our heavenly Father (*Matthew* 18:19). So be it.

Si 'the Spaniard' imagines how this would look. Addressing a 2023 Red Pill Day conference in England, he asks,...

> "How do you get your sovereignty if all these corporations are in the way? What if, when corporations use the Earth for whatever purposes they use it, you are supposed to benefit from that in some way, shape, or form? What if your Birth Certificate is actually a share certificate, and you are supposed to receive distributions or dividends from the trade that is being allowed to take place on your Earth, often with the resources of the Earth which belong to you? You've got Dominion over it. This is your property, it's every man's property.
>
> "So if corporations are using your property to make profit and gain, surely things should be operating from

> the perspective that the government is there to ensure that: first, only corporations that benefit Man get a licence to operate, and can operate on that legal platform; and second, only corporations that don't pollute the Earth or poison Man can operate and get a licence—it's got to be for the betterment of Man—and that those corporations must be paying the taxes because those taxes can then finance any public servants, if we need to finance them in that way, but otherwise, any profits can then be distributed to Man, which means that Man wouldn't have to work... That's the way that it should be working, and it could be working."

But what do we have now instead? Broadcaster and 'Health Ranger' Mike Adams nails it in a May 2024 broadcast...

> "Taxation is theft, taxation is confiscation, taxation is stealing the product of your labor, forcing you to hand over the product of your work, your sweat and tears and ideas and physical labor and whatever else you put into your job. The fact that, effectively, taxation is now well over 50% of your income—far beyond that, it's more like 70% if you start adding it all up, and in some cases, even higher.
>
> "Even in America, think about it, 70-plus percent taxation rates between property taxes, sales taxes, income taxes, social-security taxes, on and on and on, state and federal income taxes. That is stealing, or

confiscating, the product of your labor, which is just another form of slavery...

"If you're working for anybody in 2024, you do not own 70% of the product of your labor, and the 30% that you are allowed to keep is losing value every day because the government's stealing even more value by printing more money every single day.

"So really, slavery has just expanded to encompass everyone. We're all enslaved by this current system, and finding freedom in this world today is incredibly difficult. Finding financial freedom or even financial privacy is incredibly difficult. Finding freedom to speak is incredibly difficult... Think about how enslaved you are if you're not allowed to speak, you're not allowed to assert ownership over your own body, and you're not allowed to keep the vast majority of the product of your effort. That's slavery, folks. That is total, wholesale slavery. That's what exists in our world today."

Hear too, the righteous rant of a 'common man', in a widely circulated video post, after he received a bill from the Internal Revenue Service (IRS)..."

"I don't have any money because you're taking 60% of what I make through my LLC and absolutely crushing small businesses. And on top of that, the only reason I'm a small business is because, during the imagination period of the 'flu scare of 2019 until fucking forever, I guess, you mandated that I take an imagination shot that I didn't need and no-one knew anything about, and

> if I didn't take it, you took my fucking career away from me. You took my ability to feed my child. You took that away from me, and for two years, I have sold T-shirts in parking lots and I have worked this dead-end job at a gun store, and I have cut trees and mowed lawns and done anything I could, everything I had to do, just to feed my child. Not vacations, not new clothes, not a new truck, not thriving in my life, not living in my life, just surviving day to day. And if I don't pay you $700, I go to jail? What is slavery then?!"

Brothers and Sisters, we were not put on this Earth to carry such burdens. As Canadian builder and tax refuser Dean Clifford said in a 2013 interview,...

> "Government is too big. They take in too much money, they waste too much money. It's not my duty or my obligation to fund a bloated, ineffective governmental structure. They can downsize, they can provide us with the essential services that they were mandated to provide us in the first place. The gasoline taxes pay for the roads. Importing and exporting tariffs, excise taxes, and things like royalties paid on the resources that are mined, forested, or fished, are supposed to pay for the essential services. Why is it my responsibility to keep giving them more money because they can't live within their mandate? It's not. It's actually my duty to cut them off when I think they're being irresponsible."

Government Racketeering

Taxes amount to protection rackets. In the words of Australian commentator and prophet Max Igan, in a June 2024 broadcast,...

> "These are not governments, these are criminal enterprises, all of them are criminal enterprises. That's just the nature of Government, isn't it? Criminal racketeering is what best describes our governments. People pay protection money in the form of taxes, play registration, all this sort of stuff. This is all just protection money, it's all just racketeering. 'You register your business and you pay your taxes, or we'll come and do bad things to you.' Mob mentality, folks, it's mob racketeering."

Yes, 'registration' is part of the racket too, wherein you sign your assets over to the government, from your house to your car to your children, and even your backyard chickens. So bear in mind, as Alan of Salisbury puts it in a 2016 lecture, "When you register something, you are giving away whatever you are registering to whoever you are registering it with."

Pharisees and Religion

I have described taxation as an affront to Nature, but it is also an affront to the Creator of Nature and to the Word through whom all things were made (*John* 1:3). Those who would impose it stand accused of the crime with which Jesus charged the Pharisees of his day: "They tie up heavy loads and put them on men's shoulders but do not lift a finger to help them" (*Matthew* 23:4). It is a bloated tithe paid to a cult religion called 'Government', which then uses it to fund our demise and destruction.

Through taxation, we are treated as lifelong criminals paying a perpetual debt to society. The idea of being inherently and incurably criminal infects churches too, which is why preachers have such an obsession with 'sin' and with the idea that we were born into sin and must go around calling ourselves 'sinners', even though Scripture confers righteousness on those who have put their faith in Christ. It even calls us "slaves to righteousness" (*Romans* 6:18) who have the Mind of Christ (*1 Corinthians* 2:16), and the True Law written in our hearts (*Hebrews* 8:10).

But it's very convenient to the state if it can get you to think of yourself as a perpetual sinner because then you will more readily accept being a permanent debtor and permanent taxpayer. Then it can place even more burdens on you, dictate what rituals you must perform, what payments you must make, what medicines you must take, to be deemed acceptable to society.

It's a counterfeit righteousness designed to weigh you down all your life, and they've got you paying indulgences in the form of taxes because the state regards itself as your priest. Thus, it imposes its rules and 'mandates' and pretends that these are for your good or the good of society. Even if you do follow their rules, these parasites will shift the goalposts on you anyway to catch you out and criminalize you. They will bleed you dry if they can, while inventing yet more capricious burdens for you to carry, until you can carry burdens no more and are discarded onto the scrapheap of medical waste.

Taxation Crucified

It is time, therefore, to stop bending the knee to false authority. I can't speak for you, but my only authority is Jesus, Yeshua, who "cancelled the written code, with its regulations, that was against us and that stood opposed to us; he took it away, nailing it to the cross" (*Colossians* 2:14).

Of all the brilliant things the apostle Paul wrote, this one I treasure most. Another is where he likens our freedom from legal obligation to that of a widow set free from any obligation she had to her former husband (*Romans* 7:2). In our ignorance and folly, we were once wedded to a nagging husband called 'Government', and we tried to appease him with our offerings, our confessions, our deference, and our fear. We did not realize we were bound to a phantom, a dead thing, a fiction fashioned by men, but now, we laugh at this lifeless idol demanding our obedience, at the false priests waving it in our face, and at their false doctrines and legal writ masquerading as Law.

All that is dead to us now. We are set free from the struggle for what Martin Luther calls 'civic righteousness' in his *Commentary on the Book of Galatians* (1535) and from any need to be deemed righteous in the eyes of the state. Rather, true righteousness is "a mere passive righteousness," the righteousness that comes by faith and faith alone, and requires no tax to obtain it. In short,...

TAXATION IS DEAD TO US!

And we are dead to it, for we have let our false, corporate, STRAWMAN-self be lost that we may find our true, three-dimensional self (*Matthew* 16:25) as a Living Man or Living Woman. The old has gone, the new has come (2 *Corinthians* 5:17), and like new wine in old wineskins or new cloth patched onto old clothing, we tear the old structures trying to contain us (*Mark* 2:21-22).

What is that old cloth made of? To fully untangle the litany of deceit perpetrated by governments, bankers, and secret societies over the centuries would require several books. It includes the *Cestui Que Vie Act*, passed in England in 1666 after the Great Fire of London, that deems us legally dead. It includes man-made legalities that treat us as livestock in a tax farm and fraudulently call themselves Law. It includes enrolment into bondage through the Birth Certificate, social-security numbers, payroll deductions, and other desecrations of Privacy, and it involves deceptive contracting ploys that presume our tacit consent to be oppressed and enslaved. All these wheels of extortion have been greased by fear-mongering, propaganda, and indoctrination.

And speaking of indoctrination, I would like to know

who crowbarred into the Bible what I call *The Tyrant's Charter* in *Romans* 13:1-7, a passage falsely attributed to the apostle Paul. It tells us to obey Earthly authorities and pay taxes, notions not only at odds with the rest of the Bible but with Paul's own life and teachings. It is a naked attempt to corral Christians into obeying political powerbrokers, not the output of Paul's pen but fruit from a poison tree.

Common Law and Magna Carta

Also affronted by taxation is Common Law which, in accordance with Christ's Commandment to love others as we love ourselves, boils down to doing no harm, being honorable in contracts, and Presumption of Innocence. Where there is no victim, there is no crime. Where there is no crime, there is no fine, much less a lifelong penance to pay in the form of taxation. Along with other revenue-raising schemes of governments, courts, and police, taxation is an abomination in the eyes of Common Law which upholds our Right to keep the private property that we exchanged for our labour.

That taxation is inherently unlawful is even acknowledged at times in the documents of men. *Magna Carta* states, "No free man shall be seized or imprisoned, or stripped of his rights or possessions, or outlawed or exiled, or deprived of his standing in any other way, nor will we proceed with force against him, or send others to do so, except by the lawful judgement of his equals or by the law of the land" (Article 39). And England's *Bill of*

Rights (1688/1689) states, "... any forfeiture before conviction is illegal and void."

The spirit of this language echoes in the Fifth Amendment to the Constitution of the States United where none may be "deprived of life, liberty, or property, without due process of law." (I say, 'States United' both to distinguish the nation from the corporate fiction that has usurped the name, 'United States', and because it more accurately encapsulates the nation's true and original standing.) Furthermore, the protections of *Magna Carta* and the *Bill of Rights* carry over through the Ninth Amendment: "The enumeration in the Constitution, of certain rights, shall not be construed to deny or disparage others retained by the people."

Governments argue, of course, that *Magna Carta* no longer applies or that it applies only in part, demonstrating that they are evil, stupid, or illiterate, probably all three, for it states, "... men in our kingdom shall have and keep all these liberties, rights, and concessions, well and peaceably in their fullness and entirety for them and their heirs, of us and our heirs, in all things and all places for ever" (Article 63). Thus, *Magna Carta* has sealed itself against future dilution, adulteration, or expiry. What part of "fullness," "entirety," and "for ever" do they not understand?

Legislation Is Dead to Us

Once we revert to our true standing, governments, legislatures, and courts, which are all corporations, along with their various departments, agencies, and enforcers, will have to acknowledge that we are 'non-statutory', meaning not subject to legislation nor to the taxation they would derive from it. Nor shall we let tyranny's fabric call itself 'Law'. The idea that any order or document issued by men can be called 'Law' is absurd, laughable, and blasphemous by pretending to play God who is the only Law-giver. Trying to apply such instruments to a Living Man or Living Woman is like trying to wound the wind with a sword or to stab water, to paraphrase from Shakespeare's *The Tempest* (III.iii.).

As Mike Colomb, founder of The Renegade Nation (therenegadenation.org) explains, statutory legislation "only deals with millions of man-made 'code' violations related to 'juristic' fiction entities with their names spelled in all-capital letters, and where in any legal dispute with the I.R.S., there is never an actual 'harmed' living man or woman."

Furthermore, acts, statutes, and tax codes are merely corporate contracts that one party has drafted, one party has read, one party has negotiated with itself, and one party has signed. Yet that party thinks to impose this contract on another party, us, without our signature or consent. That is fraud.

Therefore, we no longer play along with corporate theatre nor pay homage to the things of men, for that would be idolatry. Rather, we regard ourselves, and refer to ourselves, as Man, Woman, or perhaps National, and shun corporate titles such as 'citizen', 'person', 'driver', 'inhabitant', or 'taxpayer'. Nor are we 'federal', 'fiduciary', 'juristic', or 'statutory'.

Court Precedent

Several court precedents also underline our Common-Law instincts when it comes to taxation. In 1906, the U.S. Supreme Court stated in Hale v. Henkel that an individual's rights...

> "existed by the law of the land long antecedent to the organization of the state, and can only be taken from him by due process of law, and in accordance with the Constitution. Among his rights are a refusal to incriminate himself, and the immunity of himself and his property from arrest or seizure except under a warrant of the law. He owes nothing to the public so long as he does not trespass upon their rights."

In 1931, the Oregon Supreme Court ruled, in Redfield v. Fisher,...

> "The individual, unlike the corporation, cannot be taxed for the mere privilege of existing. The corporation is an artificial entity which owes its existence and charter powers to the state; but the individual's rights to live and own property are natural rights for the enjoyment of which an excise cannot be imposed."

Then there's a Tennessee Supreme Court ruling of

1960, in Jack Cole Co. v. MacFarland, that "Realizing and receiving income or earnings is not a privilege that can be taxed... Since the right to receive income or earnings is a right belonging to every person, this right cannot be taxed as a privilege."

Courts have said similar about fees demanded by governments, which are really just another form of taxation. In 1943, the U.S. Supreme Court stated in Murdock v. Pennsylvania, "A State may not impose a charge for the enjoyment of a right granted by the Federal Constitution."

In Closing...

You may think me presumptuous to argue we owe no taxes to Government, though you will admit I have *made* an argument, not just asserted this. But in reality, the only presumption here is that of the state in supposing it has a right to demand tax from us in the first place. It doesn't.

Nor can we expect the system to repair itself and deal with us more justly. If you have been with me throughout this *Battle Manuals for Freedom series*, you will know that I don't see any solution to tyranny, financial or otherwise, through the political mechanisms now in place.

Nor do I look to vote in a fake saviour nor to install a de-facto king who will preside over a dictatorship posing as democracy. Heed the prophet Samuel's warning to the elders of Israel, that such a man will take the best of your possessions and give them to his cronies, "and you yourselves will become his slaves" (*1 Samuel* 8).

In the words of Larken Rose,...

> "The Left will rob you and dominate you; the Right will rob and dominate you. They will take turns robbing and dominating you, and you keep voting for it as if you're making a difference. How many hundreds of years have to go by of that happening before you realize this isn't really fixing anything?"

So, what other fixes are available to us? That is my theme in the following chapter.

2

A TAX DETOX

And let Jerusalem and her environs, her tithes and her revenues, be holy and free from tax… No-one shall have authority to exact anything from them or annoy any of them about any matter… Let them live by their own laws.

— *1 MACCABEES* 10:31,35,37

What, then, is the least burdensome way to shed the tax burdens of men? It's not that complicated. You note the Crimes against Humanity perpetrated by the government pretending to represent you, and you refuse to incriminate yourself by giving it your financial support.

In the words of Canadian activist and Man of God, Kevin Annett, who has waged a long campaign against the atrocities of church and state in Canada,…

> "If you're a citizen of a country that's practising war crimes, you are obligated not to pay taxes and not to follow the [statutes] of that regime, because then you're colluding, and in fact, as an individual, you have a responsibility to bring charges against your own country, your own regime that's doing this."

This view is reinforced by Chris Coverdale, a former fraud investigator and now activist, who points out that in September 2001, the U.K. Parliament ratified the *Rome Statute* of the International Criminal Court (1998) with the *International Criminal Court Act*. This legislation specifies prison sentences for up to 30 years for conduct ancillary to genocide, war crimes, and Crimes Against Humanity. That conduct, as Coverdale explains in a 2022 interview with British broadcaster Richard Vobes, includes *funding* the crimes.

Coverdale also cites the *International Convention for the Suppression of the Financing of Terrorism*, adopted by the General Assembly of the United Nations in 1999. By October 2018, according to Wikipedia, the treaty had been ratified by 188 states. Paying taxes cannot be legal under this statute because it finances terrorism. Even if the national government of your country has not sent troops to crush other peoples, destroy their infrastructure, or steal their natural resources, it has for sure perpetrated medical genocide at home, as I amply demonstrate in *Know Your Medical Rights*. In short,...

PAYING TAXES IS A CRIMINAL ACT!

"On Oct. 7, 2001, Tony Blair told us that we were starting to attack Afghanistan," Coverdale said in another interview with journalist Gordon Dimmack, "so anything you have paid in tax since Oct. 7, 2001 has been a criminal offence." (TikTok appears to have silenced the video clip, but you can still read the subtitles.)

Coverdale does not pay income tax himself. Nor does he pay council tax—equivalent to property tax—because, since 1787, council-tax revenues have gone into the same 'Consolidated Fund' of the national government as its other revenues, meaning they are used to fund the same atrocities.

Tax Rebellion

Coverdale's strategy has a power that petitions and protests will never have because we'll never persuade psychopaths to put themselves in someone else's shoes, get a soul transplant, or otherwise change their behaviour. His studies of successful revolutions throughout history, including *Magna Carta*, convinced him that every major change in society started with tax rebellion. To that end, he works with two key strategies I discuss in *Know Your Lawful Rights*: 1/ Turning the legislation of tyrants back against them—I'll call it 'boomeranging' legislation; and 2/ Conditional Acceptance.

Though it is true that governments and parliaments write legislation to extort, enslave, and exterminate the populations they purport to represent, occasionally some good stuff gets through. After all, evil-doers will wear devotion's visage and pious action to "sugar o'er the devil himself," as Shakespeare said (*Hamlet*, III.i), and the devil himself masquerades as an angel of light while his servants masquerade as servants of righteousness (2 *Corinthians* 11:13-15). That means we can always find something in their disingenuous texts to boomerang against them.

Even so, we need to be smart about our non-compliance. Coverdale advises putting the funds that governments or their agencies expect from us into 'Trust'. In basic terms, a 'Grantor' sets up a Trust to benefit a Beneficiary, and the one entrusted to carry this out is a Trustee. Coverdale suggests you set aside the funds a taxing entity expects from you, call it a Trust, and name the taxing entity as the Primary Beneficiary.

Now, this is where Conditional Acceptance comes in: you declare to that entity that the funds are being held in Trust and will be released on Condition that they supply Proof, by the end of the financial year, that no funds have been used for criminal purposes. You will also require from them Proof that criminal proceedings are underway against those responsible for illegal wars, experimental vaccination campaigns, or other atrocities you name. You can write the amount on a cheque which you retain in the interim.

Being criminal to the core, the various extractors from the People's purse cannot and will not meet the Burden of Proof by the end of the financial year, after which the funds go to a Secondary Beneficiary, most likely you. This

Conditional-Acceptance strategy avoids getting into a Controversy on which a court could rule though, as Coverdale points out, the false authorities are not keen to take him to court because he would be proved right and that would set a highly inconvenient precedent for them.

With Conditional Acceptance, you are not outright refusing to pay tax, but withholding payment until the criminals fall to their knees in repentance. That day may come but not until, as prophesied,...

> *"they shall be terrified,*
> *And they shall be downcast of countenance,*
> *And pain shall seize them,*
> *When they see that Son of Man*
> *Sitting on the throne of his glory."*
>
> — *FIRST BOOK OF ENOCH*, 62:5

By then, of course, it will be too late because...

> *"the wrath of the Lord of Spirits resteth on them,*
> *And His sword is drunk with their blood."*
>
> — *FIRST BOOK OF ENOCH*, 62:12

Coverdale has drawn up a set of documents you can use in your dealings with the powers-that-shouldn't-be, including a *DECLARATION of SOVEREIGNTY and DEED of DISCRETIONARY, REVOCABLE, CONDITIONAL TRUST and WITHDRAWAL of CONSENT to ILLEGAL TAXATION.*

It's a thing of beauty, though I would replace a few instances of 'law' with 'legislation' or with 'statute' when not being used in a quotation. As I explain throughout this series, the Creator makes Law, men make legislation, and corporations write company policy. You can complete the document, sign it with witness, and send it to the troublesome corporation. (All governments, parliaments, courts, and police forces are corporations.)

Coverdale has also produced a document for employees whose earnings are taxed at source by an employer. You instruct the employer to divert all pay-as-you-earn and National-Insurance deductions into a Trust payable only when the government has ceased its crimes and is acting lawfully. You instruct the employer that, until these conditions are met, its trustees are to "return all such payments to the employees." All these documents are available, along with instructions, at https://www.probityco.com/.

Or you can write your own documents, which is always my preference. By doing so, you will stand upon a surer foundation. You confirm to yourself and others that you have grasped the subject matter, and thwart the ready comeback of extortioners that you just copied something off the Internet. That's why I have favoured presenting you with information and concepts that you can adapt for yourself, rather than one-size-fits-all templates.

A simpler variation on Coverdale's theme comes from Allegedly Dave, a self-described "ordinary bloke from Basildon in Essex," who told podcaster and presenter James Delingpole in a September 2024 interview that he also makes tax payment conditional on the government proving that it is not funding terrorism, but he doesn't bother with a Trust.

Nor does the 'People's Lawyer', David Adelman, who points out that HM Revenue & Customs (HMRC) need to contract with us to exact any tax payment. "You only become a taxpayer by consent and by contract," he told Richard Vobes during a March 2024 live stream. The same goes for taxing entities in other countries. "If you do not fill in and sign a tax return, you are not in contract, and if you are not in contract, there is no obligation, end of."

Adelman has not been troubled by HMRC since he pointed this out to them in 2015. "If they have no paperwork—in other words, no evidence of contract—they cannot pursue it. There's nothing to pursue."

Revocation of Consent in the States United

If you are dwelling in the States United, another approach is to send the Internal Revenue Service (IRS) an Affidavit revoking any Consent it assumes you have given to file and pay taxes.

This is founded on a realignment of status, both yours and the government's. You are a Living Man or Woman with authority over Government. To put that in official terms even a bureaucrat could understand, you are a 'nontaxpayer'. Quoting the District Court of Montana in the famous 1922 case, Long v. Rasmussen—with the proviso that 'laws' should read 'legislation',...

> "The revenue laws are a code or system in regulation of tax assessment and collection. They relate to taxpayers, and not to nontaxpayers. The latter are without [outside] their scope. No procedure is prescribed for nontaxpayers, and no attempt is made to annul any of their rights and remedies in due course of law. With them Congress does not assume to deal, and they are neither of the subject nor of the object of the revenue laws."

This language was echoed by the United States Court of Claims in 1972 in Economy Plumbing & Heating v. United States.

As for the government's status, by its own admissions it is a foreign corporation with zero jurisdiction outside the District of Columbia (DC). According to the *United States Code* (*USC*), a compilation of legislation organized by subject matter, the term 'United States' is defined as "a Federal corporation" (Title 28, Section 3002 (15)(a)).

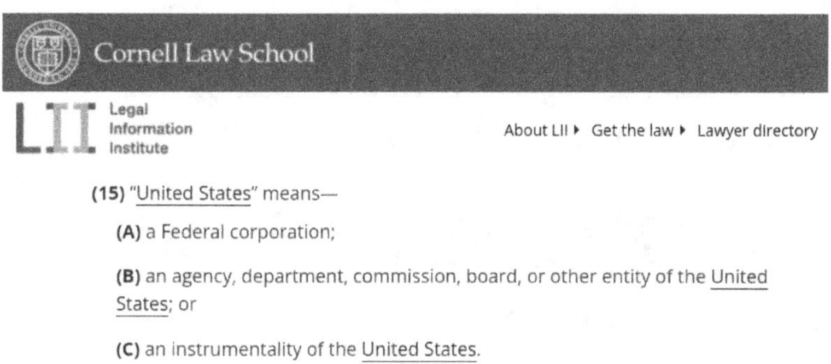
Cornell Law School

LII Legal Information Institute

About LII ▸ Get the law ▸ Lawyer directory

(15) "United States" means—

(A) a Federal corporation;

(B) an agency, department, commission, board, or other entity of the United States; or

(C) an instrumentality of the United States.

And said corporation is located in DC, according to

the *Uniform Commercial Code* (*UCC*, §9-307(h)), a body of legislation that governs commercial transactions.

Cornell Law School

LII Legal Information Institute

(h) [Location of United States.]

The United States is located in the District of Columbia.

What, then, is the relationship between that corporation in DC and the States of the Union? Foreign! As described in *Corpus Juris Secundum*, an encyclopaedia of legislation, "The United States government is a **foreign** corporation with respect to a State" (Vol. 19, Section 883, emphasis mine).

As for the IRS itself, the clue is in the name. As an 'internal' revenue service, not an external one, its jurisdiction is confined to the 10-square-mile foreign enclave of DC. It is also a foreign trust domiciled in Puerto Rico, as set out in Title 31, Section 1321 of the USC ((a) (62)).

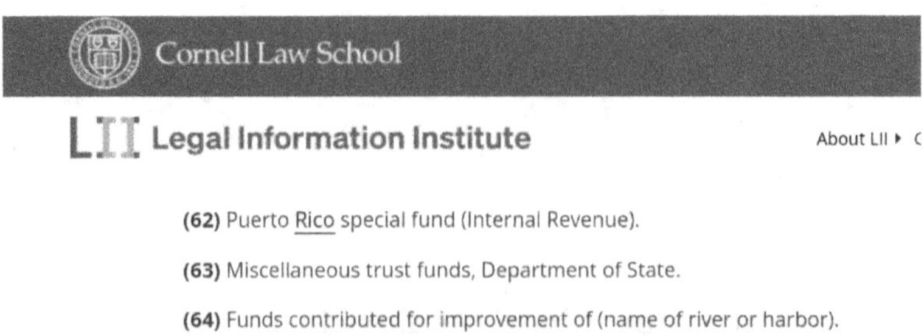
Cornell Law School

LII Legal Information Institute About LII ▸ C

(62) Puerto Rico special fund (Internal Revenue).

(63) Miscellaneous trust funds, Department of State.

(64) Funds contributed for improvement of (name of river or harbor).

Brothers and Sisters, you and I owe no allegiance to a corporation, much less a foreign one! According to Mike Colomb of The Renegade Nation, IRS agents should register as foreign agents with respect to States of the Union, in order to comply with the *Foreign Agents Registration Act* (1938), and as foreign debt collectors with secretaries of State to conform with the *Fair Debt Collection Practices Act* (1971). Having failed to do either, they are no better than illegal debt collectors, and the IRS is "an illegal debt-collection company" that is "violating too many laws to mention if or when they attempt to impose their foreign tax laws on you."

Paying U.S. Income Tax Is Voluntary.

By now, you will observe that I am deep into legislation, not Law, though Colomb mistakenly calls it law, so I'll say again that legislation is not written for us but for Government officials and employees, and that we cite it selectively only to hold *them* to *their* contractual obligations. The legislation in play here is the *Internal Revenue Code* (*IRC*), which forms Title 26 of *USC*.

At first glance, Section 7201 of that Title looks scary, but that's what tyrants do, trying to rule by fear and intimidation, and they have been honing this dark art for thousands of years:

> "Any person who willfully attempts in any manner to evade or defeat any tax imposed by this title or the payment thereof shall, in addition to other penalties

> provided by law, be guilty of a felony and, upon conviction thereof, shall be fined not more than $100,000 ($500,000 in the case of a corporation), or imprisoned not more than 5 years, or both, together with the costs of prosecution."

But let's break it down. To begin with, I hope by now that you do not identify as a 'PERSON' living in the fictional realm of Legal Land, a place no more real than Legoland or Toytown. Nor are you a character in some kind of fairground installation.

Even the definition of 'person' in the IRC is circular, saying it includes, "an officer or employee of a corporation, or a member or employee of a partnership, who as such officer, employee, or member is under a duty to perform the act in respect of which the violation occurs."

This is nothing more than saying the Code applies to those "under a duty to perform the act." In other words, it applies to whom it applies. It matters to whom it matters. And, to whom does it apply? To whom does it matter? **Only those who have voluntarily agreed to it, as confirmed in** many statements by U.S. government officials and by former IRS agent, Joseph Banister.

Banister was forced out of the agency in 1999 after he asked inconvenient questions about the true obligations of people living in the States. "There's no law that makes the average American required to file these returns and pay the income tax," he told broadcaster Vincent James in an August 2024 interview.

That's why, according to Colomb, the U.S. Treasury does not define payments received as 'income taxes' but as 'Donations' to the Treasury. You unwittingly agreed to make these voluntary donations by filling out a *1040* form in the past, but these were in effect confessions by which you ceded your Fifth-Amendment Right to Remain Silent and gave IRS a jurisdiction it has no right to have.

Taxation and the Constitution.

I have talked about constitutions before and how they are generally accorded higher authority than other legislation. For the most part, they are lawful, in that they enshrine the ways we want to be protected and agree to protect others, in accordance with Christ's Commandment to love others as we love ourselves. But ultimately, they are still legislation, not law, for they are written and revised by men. Men cannot be law-makers, any more than they can write, revise, or repeal the laws of motion or of thermodynamics. Even half-wit Freemasons can write what they call constitutions, though they are abominations in the eyes of Man and of the Most High.

Therefore, I parse out from constitutions that which is beneficial and therefore lawful, from that which is harmful and therefore unlawful. When it comes to the *Constitution* of the States United, I will retain the *Bill of Rights,* which is the first ten Amendments to the Constitution, and reject some of the language added later to enslave us.

Who am I to do this? A Living Man, and Living Men

and Living Women have Dominion of the Earth and authority over the ephemeral creations of men. The Sixteenth Amendment, wherein Congress assumed "power to lay and collect taxes on incomes," was not added until 1913, and even then, it was never ratified by the States.

Several Supreme-Court decisions in the following years ruled, as in Stanton v. Baltic Mining Co. (1915/1916), that, "The provisions of the Sixteenth Amendment conferred no new power of taxation." As reported in *The New York Times* on Jan. 25, 1916, "In substance, the court holds that the Sixteenth Amendment did not empower the Federal Government to levy a new tax."

Much of this historical background is set out in the documentary film, *Freedom to Fascism,* where tax attorney Peter Gibbons states,...

> "Congress tried to enact an income tax in 1894. The Supreme Court said that's unconstitutional. When the Supreme Court says something is unconstitutional, it's unconstitutional. They tried again in 1913, and the Supreme Court said the Sixteenth Amendment conferred no new power of taxation. So if they didn't have it then, and they didn't get it, they don't have it. There is no constitutional basis for a tax on the wages of Americans living and working in the 50 states of the Union. Period. End of argument."

Still, we may mark down 1913 as a bad year for the

States United, not just because of the Sixteenth Amendment but because it was also when the U.S. government introduced an income tax and *Form 1040*. Also, as we shall see in a later chapter, it was when the *Federal Reserve Act* was passed.

What this boils down to is that you have been handing over the fruit of your toil without obligation to do so. Colomb recommends that, armed with this knowledge, you send the IRS a witnessed letter/Affidavit affirming your status as a Living Man or Woman and nontaxpayer and letting this foreign corporation know you do not consent to paying income tax, nor to any presumption or inference of consent by the IRS. You no longer volunteer to donate your private property to a foreign treasury, effective immediately, nor to file a *1040* form, and you require the IRS to note in its own files, records, and databases that you are a nontaxpayer.

You also notify IRS that if it wishes to dispute any part of your Affidavit, it must do so within x number of days with a point-by-point rebuttal, an option which, in practice, the IRS never pursues. Its failure to rebut or challenge your Affidavit in that time frame acts as a legal default ('estoppel'), and your sworn declaration stands as Truth in Law.

My own Affidavit to the IRS is below. If you choose to do similar, I urge you still to write your own…

Daniel Werfel
Commissioner, Internal Revenue Service
1111 Constitution Avenue NW
Washington, DC 20224

Name—Affidavit Affirming Non-Taxable Status

1/ My name is _____________, a Living Man. I was allegedly born in ___________ on _____________.

2/ I am writing to inform IRS that I, as a Living Man without residence in the District of Columbia (DC), am not required to pay income tax and will not do so.

3/ Nor am I subject, in conducting business in my name or any other, to any levy, tax, or regulation originating from DC, nor from any other government, agency, or corporation.

4/ Furthermore, I am under no obligation to provide financial data or produce filings to IRS or any other DC or foreign entity, and will not knowingly do so.

5/ For your purposes, I am a 'non-taxpayer', and I require that IRS make any necessary adjustments to its files, records, and databases to accord with this.

> 6/ I do not consent to any assumption, presumption, or inference that contradicts the above, either by IRS or any other government body or corporation, foreign or domestic.
>
> If IRS wishes to dispute this Notice, it has 40 days from this date to do so in writing to the above address, after which time it shall stand as Truth in Law.

I signed this Affidavit with Witness, copied it, and sent it by Recorded Delivery in 2023. I have not heard anything back since.

Once we issue such a Notice, none may bring an accusation of tax 'evasion' against us because we stand firm in the Truth that we were never required to pay tax in the first place. Any subsequent attempt by the IRS to collect taxes—any letter, form, notice, or demand—amounts to mail fraud and is punishable with a 30-year prison sentence under the *Privacy Act* and prosecution under the *Racketeer Influenced and Corrupt Organizations (RICO) Act*.

In the event IRS attempts legal action, I can inform the tax court of my nontaxpayer status and deny it any jurisdiction. Colomb reports that the tax court in D.C. is dismissing IRS claims on that basis. Meanwhile, the Affidavit does not in any way detract from any government benefit program to which we are entitled, such as Social Security or Medicare, whether now or in the future.

If you don't want to be so 'in-your-face' about it, you

can favour the Conditional-Acceptance approach. Whenever you receive some Notice or demand from this foreign corporation, you can start asking the questions you know they cannot answer: By what law am I required to file or pay income tax? Show me where I signed any legislation you cite. Provide Proof that the Sixteenth Amendment was ratified. Prove that IRS has any jurisdiction outside the District of Columbia. Prove that no IRS revenue is funding crimes deemed illegal under the *Rome Statute* of the International Criminal Court. And so on.

David E. Robinson also gives sound advice in *The UCC Connection*:

> "NEVER ARGUE THE FACTS IN A TAX CASE. [MAXIM: 'ARGUMENTS ARE FOR FOOLS'.] If you're not required to file, what do you care whether they say you owe sixty dollars or 60,000 dollars. If you are not required to file, the amount doesn't matter. DON'T ARGUE THE AMOUNT… The minute you say, 'I don't owe that much,' you have voluntarily agreed that you owe them something, and you have just given them jurisdiction."

Fines Are Taxes Too

Close cousin to taxation are fines, devised to extract yet more of your lifeforce by penalizing you for some infringement of corporate code, even though you have done no harm. A powerful way to deal with this, as

Allegedly Dave explained to Delingpole, is to start out with the obvious truth that he who makes an allegation must produce the Proof. For example, if a speeding infraction is alleged, a photograph taken by a speed camera is not sufficient to prove you were driving a particular car at a particular time on a particular day at a particular speed. For one thing, there is no first-hand witness to the purported event. Furthermore, measurement of distances and speeds can be incorrectly calibrated, photographs can be doctored and airbrushed, and Automatic Number Plate Recognition (ANPR) systems have a high error rate.

Dave points out, "You can legitimately say, and honestly say, 'I have no record of being at that place at that time on that day. Can you provide me some evidence that I was there?' " A camera is not a witness and therefore not primary evidence. He also argues it is highly unlikely this approach will end up in court because, if it did, you would ask, "Where's the evidence I asked for?" They won't be able to provide it, and "the case is gone."

How can a computer bring a man to court? asks researcher Mr Blue in a September 2024 conversation with Richard Vobes. "They're supplying nothing more than a photograph of a registration plate saying this car was assumed to be speeding. Okay, show me the Proof, show me the evidence. Where are your witnesses? You have to have an independent witness to make the claim... The police or the council have to give independent evidence. It's hardly independent if it's their own bits of technology that's designed to capture people."

In Closing...

This was a tough chapter to write because most of the so-called Freedom-Movement researchers get into circular analysis of quoting each other, making it hard to break out of the loop and get back to the original sources. So many unlinked articles, so many dead ends, and so many quotes inaccurately transcribed or taken out of context. I have done my best to mitigate these shortfalls by finding the original documents, saving them, and highlighting them so that this book, like the others in this series, shall stand as a document of record.

Of the two main approaches suggested in this chapter —Coverdale's tax rebellion on the basis that taxes fund genocide, and Colomb's Revocation notice to the IRS— the former has universal appeal and requires less getting into the weeds with legislation and court precedent. It therefore appears a simpler path to accord with Christ's command to leave the Beast system termed 'Babylon': "Come out of her, my people, so that you will not share in her sins" (*Revelation* 18:4).

Simpler yet—and this is my preference—is not to bother with the Trust element and, like Allegedly Dave, go the Conditional-Acceptance path alone. In any case, the same key principle applies: If Government wants to extract your property, it must shoulder the Burden of Proof that it has lawful authority to do so, which it cannot do.

3

MORE ON COUNCIL TAX IN BRITAIN

Council tax in Britain is an abomination, not just unlawful but illegal, and if you live in another country, so are *your* property taxes, but British people are beginning to turn the tide.

Veronica Chapman

Among them is Veronica: of the Chapman family. In August 2024, she released an exchange of letters with Portsmouth City Council after they demanded council tax from her. She used a combination of Conditional Acceptance and boomeranging legislation. Near the end of this exchange, Veronica answers questions with a question, an approach I also talk about in *Know Your Lawful Rights*.

In her preface to the series, Veronica explains how prosecutor and judge are the same when councils take people to court for nonpayment of council tax. This is because councils print court Summonses "on their own printers, using a letterhead that is a facsimile of the Court's letterhead." Then they rent magistrates' courts to rubber-stamp hundreds of fake Liability Orders on an industrial scale.

The exchange between Veronica and the council is a fun read if you have the time, but here's the gist. It begins with the council sending Veronica a bill for £53.19 for Apr. 1, 2020 to Mar. 31, 2021, plus £79.01 for arrears from previous years.

Veronica replies in a letter dated Mar. 14, 2020 that if the council wants her to pay anything, "Then you'd need to send a proper Invoice, constructed as per the Bills of Exchange Act 1882, **and defining the VAT situation**" (all emphases hers). She stresses that she is not refusing to pay, but "**I am making an offer to pay conditional on the other party fulfilling their obligation under the Bills of Exchange Act 1882 for this alleged charge.**" This legislation, she adds, requires the council to issue and deliver "**an invoice signed in wet ink by an officer of the company/council**..."

A couple of weeks later, one Louise Chapman from the council's revenues & benefits department writes back. To avoid any confusion, we'll just call her 'Louise' as the two antagonists share the same last name of Chapman though they are not related. Louise asserts Veronica's "liability" began in 2016 and that, "For every financial year a billing authority must serve a notice in writing on every liable person in accordance with regulations and legislation contained in the local government finance act 1992."

To which Veronica replies, "I would be happy to make a payment as soon as I receive a lawful Invoice." She points out that the *Local Government Finance Act* (1992) does not allow exemption from the *Bills of Exchange Act* (1882).

Then, in an Apr. 23, 2020 letter, Louise counters, "you are being charged in accordance with the Local Government Finance Act 1992" and, "The legislation you quote does not apply to council tax administration." Then she issues the first threat. "Failure to pay in accordance with any reminder notice may result in a summons being issued to apply to the court for a liability order to be issued."

Veronica writes back asking if the demand for payment is...

> 1/ in exchange for goods and/or services provided by the council, in which case the *Bills of Exchange Act* applies and "in consequence, I need a LAWFUL Bill for this EXCHANGE to take place LAWFULLY"; or
>
> 2/ as a punishment for convicted wrongdoing on her part, which must comply with the *Bill of Rights* (1688/89) that "all Grants and Promises of Fines and Forfeitures of particular persons before Conviction are illegall and void"; or
>
> 3/ plain extortion.

Veronica also observes in her letter that the council can print its own court summonses but "CAN'T CREATE A SIMPLE PIECE OF PAPER COMPRISING A LAWFUL INVOICE." When someone can't produce an Invoice, she continues, "it *normally* means that the demand is fraudulent."

Then Veronica points out that the legislation and regulations cited do not mention her specifically. "**None of them include my Name.** Therefore there is NO GUARANTEE THAT THEY APPLY TO ME, PERSONALLY."

Here, she invokes a truth I have been banging on about throughout this series, that Acts, statutes, and the decrees of politicians and bureaucrats are contracts written by one party that thinks to impose them on another party, you and me, without our participation, much less our signature. That is fraud. They have no jurisdiction over us whatsoever.

Then Louise ups the ante with a May 26, 2020 letter titled *Council tax appeal stage two,* where she reiterates, "we don't follow any other legislation other than Local Government Finance Act 1992." I gasped when I got to this bit. Louise is basically saying they get to pick and choose what they will and won't comply with, meaning the Executive branch is claiming authority over Parliament.

Louise goes on to list services for which council tax supposedly pays, followed by more threats: that where council tax remains unpaid, a local authority "is entitled to seek the issue of a liability order through the magistrate's court," and "Where the defendant does not appear in answer to the summons, the court may proceed in the absence of the defendant."

Louise then basically admits this so-called court is a rubber stamp enforcing extortion on behalf of the council, which then prints its own Liability Orders: "Liability orders in all cases are approved by the Magistrates and once approved are printed by Portsmouth City Council."

Veronica is quick to pounce on Louise's folly. In her May 30 reply, she queries Louise's *tax appeal stage two* heading as she has not appealed anything but is "simply asking for the lawful paperwork." Who issued this 'appeal', and when? Veronica asks, and "Who granted them Power of Attorney to do it on my behalf? Send me a copy of what they wrote... I have the Right to it as 'disclosure'."

Next, Louise writes in a letter of June 22, 2020 that what she meant to say was, "council tax complaint stage 2," not "appeal stage 2," as if that makes it any better, and that "I will not be corresponding with you any further regarding this matter but if you still disagree with my decision, please follow the appeals process as below."

In a series of letters, Veronica tells Louise she never asked her to make any decision, that the *Bills of Exchange Act* (1882) "says (in effect) that 'If no Invoice is presented, then no debt is outstanding,' " and that there is no controversy in play that would require court involvement...

> "So... once you have created your faux Court Summons (printed on Council Notepaper!), will you be writing to the Court, with copies of all my letters, so that the Court can see that the reason for the lack of funds received by the Council, **is entirely down to the fact that you have simply failed to produce the correct paperwork?**"

Or will Louise commit perjury by omission? If Louise instigates a Summons, Veronica warns she will call her as a Material Witness.

Later, the council informs Veronica it has obtained a Liability Order and, on Feb. 9, 2022, sends her a 'BROKEN ARRANGEMENT AND ENFORCEMENT WARNING NOTICE'.

In her Apr. 6, 2022 response, this time to the Borough Solicitor, Veronica demands to know what 'arrangement' had been broken and how. "You will need to provide a copy of the arrangement, which bears my signature or seal of obligation."

Then she demands a copy of the alleged Liability Order in the form of a valid Court Order. "**It will contain the LEGIBLE signature of whoever made the Order, <u>and will contain the Court Seal</u>**. She also demands a copy of the Prosecution Bundle that was used to obtain the alleged Order. Her letter is to be treated, she adds, as a Subject Access Request for any and all internal or external communications that include her name.

She closes by invoking her copyright of the name, 'AAACCEHI MNNOPRV when arranged as VERONICA

CHAPMAN', meaning, "it would cost you £ 10,000 per usage of my personal, copyrighted, logos. This would render any further 'Court Procedures' problematical (for you)."

On May 24, 2022, Louise sends various enclosures, including a purported copy of the Liability Order. Veronica sends them back a few days later, pointing out that the Liability Order is false. "If it was a REAL Court Order, it would: A) State the Order (in writing), B) State the name of the Justice or Judge making the Order (legibly!), C) Bear the signature of the Justice or Judge making the Order, D) Bear the Court Seal." The document Louise sent met none of these conditions.

"You must think I'm stupid," Veronica continues, before chastising Louise for wilfully overlooking the statutes Veronica had cited. "Just because you aren't prepared to read them, doesn't (actually) make them go away... And, if you want to emulate an ostrich, just remember which part of your anatomy will be most exposed."

Somehow, by Mar. 29, 2023, the Council had managed to put Veronica's so-called 'account' in credit but, in an Apr. 15, 2023 letter to Louise, Veronica demands...

> "a copy, signed and sealed by myself, that grants yourself, or any staff member of Portsmouth City Council, the Right to make decisions on my behalf... Then send me the Case Number of the Liability Order that you claim to have been granted, so that I can check its validity with the Ministry of Justice. Furthermore I

> am still awaiting a copy of the Prosecution bundle that was utilised in order to gain said Liability Order (bearing in mind that—according to Stones' *Justices Manual*—a Magistrates' Court has no jurisdiction to make Liability Orders)."

Louise is aghast, asking in a May 25, 2023 letter if Veronica is refusing to accept the government money issued to her council-tax account. "First of all," Veronica shoots back in a June 3, 2023 letter, "it's not 'my' council tax account. It is an account that YOU have created. **Do not** try to assign it to myself. What grants YOU Power of Attorney to raise an account, and to assign it to me?" And what gave Louise Power of Attorney to accept these funds on her behalf? "Answer those questions, and I will answer your question."

At the time of publishing, the Council was no longer in pursuit of Veronica. After all, extortioners have lower hanging fruit to collect. This is the desired result. As Veronica notes in introduction to the letter exchanges, " 'They' will NEVER admit 'defeat'. The best that can ever be achieved is 'silence'. Such that they 'leave one alone, henceforth'. They will NEVER, EVER, send a letter saying: 'Oh, yes... you were right, after all! Sorry!' No so-called 'authority' will ever do that." After Veronica published the letters, Richard Vobes did an entertaining synopsis shortly after and interviewed Veronica in August 2024.

Council-tax prosecutions that come to a so-called court are exemplars of injustice. They are conducted by what Mr Blue calls a 'pseudo court', "a fake court brought by a private corporation in the trickery of Color of Law." In his September 2024 conversation with Richard Vobes, he points out,...

> "There's no jury, nine times out of ten, no judge. It's just a panel of people sat there, and the clerk of the court is now changed from the clerk to a legal advisor, which is a corporate standing, and there's no claimant. Now, the *Bill of Rights* is very clear on this. There must be a claimant in court to make a claim. If there is no claimant, the case is dismissed. This is the problem that the council have, the police have. They cannot make a claim because they are corporate persons."

A corporation cannot bring a man to court, Mr Blue adds, because a corporation is nothing more than a piece of paper. "Can a corporation pick up a pen? No. Can a corporation sign a contract? No. Can a corporation enter the court? No."

Furthermore, the U.K. *Local Government Act* (1888) states, "All duties and liabilities of the inhabitants of a county shall become and be duties and liabilities of the council of such county" (79(2)). So, if councils suppose that council tax is owed, then that liability is theirs!

Mick Butler

Our next witness is Mick Butler from the Midlands, also interviewed by Richard Vobes. When he went to a magistrates' court over a council-tax issue with Coventry City Council, he was redirected to "the council's court."

The implications are staggering; the council has its very own court! This means that councils, as the Executive branch of local Government, have carved out for themselves an enclave within the Judiciary and become indistinguishable from it, a mockery of the Separation-of-Powers doctrine. "It's fraud," Butler told Vobes. "It's treasonous against the people."

This kangaroo-court system also falls foul of the aforementioned *Local Government Act* which forbids councils, along with their members and committees, from exercising "any of the powers of a court of record" or from performing "any judicial business" (78(2)). Yet that is exactly what councils are doing.

Butler's hearing was adjourned to a date several weeks ahead, but in the meantime, the purported court conducted a hearing about his case without informing him and, of course, found against him and issued a phantom Liability Order. When he went to the magistrate's court to find the Order, the court had no record of it, confirming that the council had issued it unilaterally. Butler's research has also confirmed that council-tax revenues in Britain go to the 'Consolidated Fund' of the national Treasury, and that every council in the U.K. is a corporation, as shown at thesovereign project.live.[1]

---

1. https://wiki.thesovereignproject.live/index.php/DUNS_-_UK_Councils

The case culminated in an appearance before a district judge. Having refused to be addressed as 'MR BUTLER' or as a 'PERSON', he told the judge, "My name is Michael, and I am representing MR MICHAEL BUTLER," then, brandishing his Birth Certificate, he declared himself the Executor and Beneficiary of that Trust.

But it was when Butler questioned the judge's Oath that he got the judge to flee the courtroom and "abandon ship." That a judge is desecrating his Oath of impartiality is not hard to demonstrate when a council has set up its own court because, in this arrangement, the judge *is* the prosecutor.

I will digress here briefly to suggest that the most powerful approach to take with any judge conspiring to take your income, property, or wealth is to attack his standing. Who is this creature clad in black who presumes to have authority here?

> *"How do I know you're a judge? I need to see your Oath and your signature on that Oath. I also demand a signed declaration that you have sworn no other secret oath, either to a Bar association or to a secret society. And I require a sworn statement that you have no financial interest in the outcome of this case."*

If the judge cannot meet all of these conditions—and we know he can't—he is IMPERSONATING A JUDGE and desecrating his public Oath. This approach strikes at the core of their fraud.

Vobes contributed his own spirited appraisal of the STRAWMAN fiction as he talked with Butler:

> "They can charge this ALL-CAPS NAME because they created this ALL-CAPS NAME. The problem they have is, this ALL-CAPS NAME doesn't have any arms or legs, doesn't breathe, and he's unable to use a pen to write a cheque out... I can only act on behalf of this thing and tell these people, 'I'm really sorry. I've spoken to this bit of paper, I've cajoled it, I've really encouraged it to pay your bill, but it's just sitting there and doing nothing.' "

Yes, imagine coming into court with a copy of your driving licence, passport, or Birth Certificate, and relaying to it every question the judge asks you, then waiting for the document to reply. After an awkward silence, you turn to the judge and say, "Well, this is awkward, but it's not giving me an answer." Or, if you're expected to stand in a particular place in a courtroom, leave a copy of your document there, or hand it to the clerk of the court and ask them to put it there for you, and inform the judge he may address his questions to it. Not so much "Talk to the hand" as "Talk to the document."

Now, extending the David-Goliath analysis I set out in *Know Your Lawful Rights* (Chapter 16), the court is really going to see double as Goliath saw double when David came down to kill him (*1 Samuel* 17:40-43).

Leighton v Bristow & Sutor

The collusion between councils and magistrates' courts was also exposed in September 2023 by a Cardiff high-court judgment in Leighton v Bristow & Sutor. Wayne Leighton filed a claim against national 'enforcement agency' Bristow & Sutor after their bailiffs set out to enforce four fake Liability Orders on behalf of York Council. He cited three statutes these corporate employees had breached—the *Tribunals and Courts Enforcement Act* (2007); the *Protection from Harassment Act* (1997); and the *Statute of Marlborough* (1267), which stipulates, "none from henceforth shall take any such Revenge or Distress of his own Authority, without Award of our Court…"

The high-court judge, named Harrison, found it troubling that, in magistrate-court proceedings dealing with council tax, "No physical individual order as such is ever actually produced by the court." Instead, the Council sends an officer with a list of Summonses, "the list is simply signed by a magistrate, and the liability order is deemed to be made." Harrison noted that on June 21, 2017 alone, the magistrates' court issued 1,474 Liability Orders in one day!

This process, the judge added, "does not identify clearly the maker of the order, and it is neither stamped, nor sealed. Further, insofar as it purports to be the basis for an award of costs, then it does not comply with the obligation to make clear whether or in what sum such costs are rewarded." He noted that, in the absence of a proper paper record of an individualized Liability Order stating the amount claimed against him, Leighton had no mechanism to appeal it. This breached Article 6 of the *European Convention on Human Rights*—Right to a fair trial.

According to the *Tribunals, Courts and Enforcement Act*, "The enforcement agent must on request show the debtor and any person who appears to him to be in charge of the premises evidence of (a) his identity, and (b) his authority to enter the premises" (Schedule 12, Paragraph 26).

Make a note of this if you are in Britain. It's important if debt collectors ever show up. Remedies are available to a debtor—including return of goods and payment of damages—when an enforcement agent "acts under an enforcement power under a writ, warrant, liability order or other instrument that is defective" (Schedule 12, Paragraph 66).

In this case, the bailiffs had refused "to provide a copy of the liability order on request, or otherwise to identify under what authority they were intending to enter his premises." Harrison also found it troubling that, in its pleadings to the court, the company said it took its authority to enter a premises from the Council. It "regarded the council's document as being the relevant authority, and furthermore, as the pleadings say, the document was carried by the agents when attending to enforce council tax liabilities." That a council, rather than a court, could authorize a contractor to enter premises and take control of goods was "problematic, to say the least."

The judge also took the defendants to task for refusing to show their authority to enter Leighton's premises; they merely told him to contact the council. Harrison wrote,...

> "In my judgment, a householder is entitled to ask the defendants on what authority they are purporting to enter his property, and the fact that they cannot do so, and refer him back, effectively to their client, is almost bound to cause him to be dissatisfied. In my judgment, the defendants are in breach of paragraph 26" (of the *Tribunals, Courts and Enforcement Act* just cited).

Harrison went on to cite the *Protection From Harassment Act,* where harassment includes "alarming the person or causing the person distress." The defendants carried out some 35 enforcement actions in various forms of contact, including email and correspondence, with 15 visits to three separate properties, including two visits to Leighton's parents. "Mr Leighton explained that the visits to the premises occupied by his parents were particularly troublesome for him. He felt that the defendants were using them as a means to get to him." Incredibly, however, the judge said the bailiffs' conduct did not meet the threshold for harassment.

In the end, Harrison awarded Leighton a paltry £4000 in damages, but it is still an important victory as it exposes and demolishes the entire council/magistrates' court charade in the U.K.

To simplify the analysis, if I assert you reneged on a promise to pay back a loan I made to you, it's not OK for me just to give some thugs a piece of paper saying I authorize them to bash your door down, much as I might want to. I have to go to court and prove that you made that promise to me in the first place and give you an opportunity to defend yourself. Only when I have satisfied the court of my case, and the court has signed a Liability Order with your name on it, stating the amount owed, and I have given you opportunity to comply with the Order and you have refused, only then do I get to enlist enforcers. But British councils are skipping all of this Due Process, making for systemic injustice.

As explained in a Substack article by The98thmonkey, "these bailiffs only showed their instructions **from the council** to enforce the debt rather than the actual proper signed authentic original order from the court." Courts have done away away with old-fashioned written Liability Orders signed by a judge "and instead ruled that the oral pronouncement of the order was all that was required, which means the enforcement companies now have a big problem to provide written proof that any order was even granted." Now that bailiffs have been caught with their pants down, it is easier to prosecute them under the *Harassment Act*.

The article includes a 'No-Trespass' notice that you can display at your property boundary. It denies 'implied right of access' to "any employee, agent, third party or representative or any other person acting on behalf of any

CORPORATE-BODY [COMPANY].” The notice also denies access to...

> “ANY POLICE-OFFICER that is acting for the CORPORATE-POLICE and not acting as expressed in their Oath of Office – ‘to serve with fairness, integrity, diligence and impartiality, upholding fundamental human rights and according equal respect to all people; and that I will, to the best of my power, cause the peace to be kept and preserved and prevent all offences against people and property.’ ”

That police forces are corporations is quickly confirmed on the U.K. government’s Companies House register. The POLICE FEDERATION OF ENGLAND AND WALES has the Company Number 04120881 and is registered as PITCOMP 233 LIMITED, a private limited company in the business of “Residents property management.”

What they mean by this, Mr Blue told Vobes, is, “We are the residents, we are the property, and they are the management.” WEST YORKSHIRE POLICE, he adds, formerly traded AS RAID-CONTROL TRUST, in the business of “Security systems service activities.” This corporation has ownership ties to debt-collection companies, “so the bailiffs are now running the police.”

In *The Council Tax Handbook*, 13th edition (2023), Child Poverty Action Group also untangle the Liability-Order fraud perpetrated by magistrates’ courts. Instead of issuing individual Liability Orders, “the judge or chair of the magistrates normally just signs a certificate attached to the list of non-payers…" In the absence of a proper stamped and sealed Order from the court,…

> "the local authority may not be able to establish that any such order exists or existed at any stage, nor show that the magistrates were ever satisfied that the local authority had proved all the matters it is required to prove… leaving local authorities to maintain records which could be wrong and incapable of independent verification. This has also been identified as a serious omission in enforcement by the High Court… The lack of an adequate and independent record may be a breach of human rights under Article 6 of the European Convention on Human Rights."

I also refer you to *The Council Tax Fraud*, an excellent analysis of tax fraud in general, and council-tax fraud in particular, at Awakened-GB (https://awakenedgb.wordpress.com/2023/04/11/the-council-tax-fraud/).

Yet another warrior in the front lines against council-tax extortion is Si the Spaniard. In a May 2024 email, he reported that "the Bailiffs have run for the hills" in a test case he was pursuing "and stated (in writing) that they will NO LONGER be seeking to execute any enforcement action on behalf of the Council concerned."

Like my other witnesses in this chapter, Si points out that the so-called courts are not issuing proper Liability Orders. "The Council simply sends a Notice stating that a 'Liability Order has been issued' - [hearsay at best]. The

Council instructed a firm of Bailiffs to go and enforce the alleged [and invisible] Liability Order."

At the time of writing, Si's team were "in hot pursuit of the Bailiffs for harassment" and for violating Schedule 12 of the *Tribunals, Courts and Enforcement Act* (2007). I shall have more to say about bailiffs in a coming chapter.

4

WEAPONIZED BANKING AND INFLATION

Where do I begin in describing the ways the banking system has exploited and enslaved us? They are many and complex and have deep historical roots. Many volumes, even entire libraries, could not encompass them all. It is easier to say how the banking system ends, so that is where I shall begin. It ends much as it ended for Pharaoh who, as told in *Exodus*, chased the People of Promise into the Red Sea and drowned, along with his army and chariots (*Exodus* 14:28). This meant liberation from slavery for the true Israelites.

Many are the parallels today with Pharaoh's Egypt. As soon as governments and media started their vaccine propaganda campaign in 2020, I saw a similarity between the needles of Big Pharma and the serpents conjured by Pharaoh's sorcerers when Moses and his brother Aaron came to Pharaoh's court (*Exodus* 7:8-13). Aaron turned his staff into a snake, and the conjurers responded by producing snakes of their own, but Aaron's snake ate theirs, signifying our victory over the enemies of the Most High.

Dodgy Dollars

Another parallel with ancient Egypt is the pyramid image on a U.S. one-dollar bill, accompanied by other occult symbols and a slogan declaring a New Order in 'Novus Ordo...'. The pyramid is also a favourite symbol of Freemasonry, indicating that secret societies run the UNITED STATES corporation, along with its servile bureaucrats in the various three-, four-, and five-letter agencies.

What else shall we say of this dollar bill? First, that being a 'fiat' currency made of paper or computer digits, it has no real value. Just as it is fraudulent to call legislation 'law', it is just as fraudulent to call this currency 'money', as it has no backing from precious metals. Both are counterfeit. As Mike Adams observes in a Mar. 12, 2024 broadcast,...

> "The dollar is a fraud. It's a currency backed by nothing and printed into oblivion by a government and a central bank that don't care about the common person, the worker, the saver, the producer. All they care about is having more power for themselves, and they create that power by printing money, which is a form of counterfeiting. They're stealing from you."

Inflation.

This theft occurs because central banks print currency to reward themselves and their conspirators first. Then, as the extra currency makes its way into circulation, it cheapens because, as basic economics dictates, the more plentiful something is, the cheaper it becomes. Thus, you will need more and more currency to buy things, meaning everything appears more expensive. You have inflation.

Inflation is therefore a form of taxation but a stealthy one because it enables governments to tax the people without them knowing. It is "legalized plunder," to quote G. Edward Griffin, famed author of *The Creature From Jekyll Island: A Second Look at the Federal Reserve*. Inflation, he told Maria Zeee in a March 2024 interview, is "manipulation of the money supply, and the legalization of that manipulation."

The Federal Reserve

Griffin's book sheds light on a massive banking conspiracy against the People, so let's talk about the 'Federal Reserve' which, as he told Zeee, "is not a government agency. It is a cartel of private banks, the biggest banks in the United States."

Griffin's assessment is underlined by the United States Court of Appeals, Ninth Circuit which concluded, in Lewis v United States of America (1982), that Federal Reserve Banks are "independent, privately owned and locally controlled corporations" (p.2).

As Griffin explains in a 1994 lecture, the Federal Reserve came into existence with the *Federal Reserve Act* of 1913. This gave us "a corporation, chartered by Congress, which was given an exclusive franchise to create the nation's money."

That so-called 'money' is conjured out of thin air when the Federal Reserve writes cheques to the U.S. government. It "springs into being precisely at the instant that the Federal-Reserve officer signs the check and gives it to the government." The government then writes cheques of its own, and the empty, meaningless dollars find their way into the private banking system and dilute the purchasing power of dollars already in circulation.

Yet how much worse has the currency printing become since Griffin gave his lecture some 30 years ago. Witness the explosion in M1, a measure of currency supply, that occurred in 2020 under the cover of COVID 'emergency'. Who, then, would disagree with Griffin's call to abolish the 'Fed', as it is called? He gives seven solid reasons…

1. It is incapable of achieving its stated objectives.
2. It is a cartel operating against the public interest.
3. It is the supreme instrument of usury.
4. It generates our most unfair tax.
5. It encourages war.
6. It destabilizes the economy.
7. It is an instrument of totalitarianism.

These traits describe central banks in general. To

quote author and Common-Law warrior Anna Maria Riezinger in a Mar. 19, 2024 article, they are…

> "useless, harmful, self-serving institutions, which do not promote peace, which do not prevent war, which do not serve humanity, which do not promote healthy economies, which do not enhance economic growth, do not improve financial stability, and do not do anything but purloin and trade upon other people's assets for their own benefit."

In *Meet Your Strawman,* David E. Robinson expresses a similar view:

> "As long as Private Central Banks are allowed to exist, inevitably—as night follows day—there will be poverty, hopelessness, and millions of deaths in endless World Wars, until the Earth itself is sacrificed to Mammon in flames. The path to true peace on Earth lies in the abolishment of all private central banking everywhere."

Fractional Reserve Banking

But the theft doesn't stop with the central banks, for now we come to the fraudulent yet 'legal' practice of 'fractional-reserve banking'. That's a big, intimidating phrase, isn't it? But all it means is that banks can lend out multiples of the amounts they have on deposit.

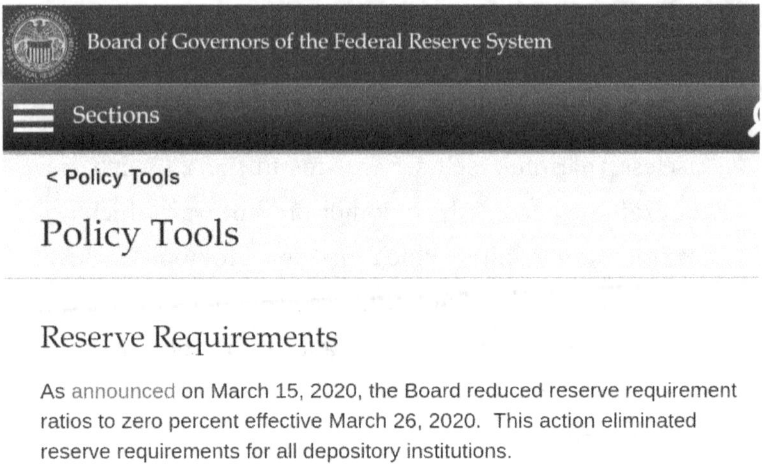

Board of Governors of the Federal Reserve System

Sections

< Policy Tools

Policy Tools

Reserve Requirements

As announced on March 15, 2020, the Board reduced reserve requirement ratios to zero percent effective March 26, 2020. This action eliminated reserve requirements for all depository institutions.

For instance, if the 'reserve requirement ratio' (RRR) is 10%, banks can lend out $100 for every $10 held in deposits. Imagine renting a storage unit in a facility that can rent out 90% of your belongings during your absence. That would be a deal-breaker, but banks do something like this, inviting the danger of bank runs when customers decide to withdraw their deposits en masse at the same time.

The RRR for U.S. banks was ten percent until, effective Mar. 26, 2020, under the cover story of 'COVID', the Fed reduced it to zero, eliminating reserve requirements entirely for all depository institutions. This was the death knell for the dollar, and demolition by design. Now, banks could lend out a trillion dollars with only a penny on deposit or nothing at all. Now, a bank's only concern when making loans is the creditworthiness of the borrower, and even that doesn't really matter because there is never a real loan in the first place. A bank need only add digits to a customer's bank account and call it a loan, without risking anything, but then the hapless customer must generate currency by his own toil to make payments which are falsely called 'repayments'.

This explains why financial institutions keep falling over themselves to make loans in times of high default. It didn't make sense to me before, but when you consider that banks collect handsomely on pretend loans that are really risk-free, and collect even more handsomely when people fall behind and have to pay additional fees, and then get to seize real assets from those who end up defaulting, it makes perfect sense. It paves the way for a few megacorporations to eventually own all assets and then rent them out to us at monopolistic prices.

Engineered Collapse?

Fiat currency "destroys every country that used it," in the words of Bill Ogden of tacticalcivics.com, interviewed by broadcaster Sarah Westall in June 2024. Back around the turn of the century, I was telling anyone who would listen that the dollar was going to collapse. Somehow, more than 20 years later, it's still limping on, but after the insane currency printing—euphemistically called 'quantitative easing'—and genocidal reserving practices ushered in with COVID, the end is surely nigh.

By now, the voices predicting dollar collapse are a swelling chorus, including Mike Adams who said in a February 2024 episode of *Situation Update*, "The systems are breaking down... Banks are going to go down, deposits are going to vanish, nations will fall." The pain will be heightened, he notes, as the dollar loses its footing as the world's 'reserve currency'.

In our lifetimes, the U.S. dollar has been the main medium of exchange for transactions between nations, but that status is eroding rapidly, especially with the emergence of a commodity-backed BRICS currency for international settlements and after Saudi Arabia announced on June 9, 2024 that it would not renew its 50-year-old agreement to trade oil exclusively in the dollar.

This means there is even less need for other nations to hold the currency, leading to increased dollar supply and accelerated decline. Then, because Americans will need to come up with more dollars to buy goods produced in other nations, domestic inflation will ramp up even more.

So the question now is not whether the dollar can be saved—too late for that—but where we go after its demise. Can we plan for honest money and transactions the other side, or will we get drawn into an even more dystopian future where worthless paper is replaced by worthless digits that can be centrally surveilled and controlled?

CBDCs

That's the dystopian nightmare presented by central-bank digital currencies (CBDC), where all transactions are conducted online using digital tokens distributed by a country's central bank or even a global central bank.

Then, without the Privacy of cash transactions, everything you buy or sell, everything you own, and everywhere you go, can be tracked and traced and linked to other information about you, such as biometric data and your medical history.

Tyrants would also have free rein to reward your behaviour and speech with extra digital spending tokens if they are pleased with you, or penalize your behaviour and speech if they are displeased, and to punish you for refusing medical directives. They could levy taxes, fees, and fines against you on a whim and give you no recourse, and if you are very naughty, cut off your funding entirely with the press of a button.

We have already seen how puppet governments and puppet banks are willing to dish out financial punishment on a whim. It was shocking to hear Canadian finance minister Chrystia Freeland announce on Feb. 14, 2022 that she would freeze the bank accounts of Canadian truckers protesting medical coercion, but I found it even more disturbing that all the financial institutions immediately obeyed her without question. Those spineless bankers presented their oiled rectums to the Canadian regime without one shred of regard for the trust placed in them by their customers to protect both their assets and their Privacy.

So, having witnessed the predatory behaviour of banks in collusion with governments, can we be in any doubt that they would seize on CBDCs as a new and devastating weapon of control?

Another benefit of CBDCs for the cabal, as pointed

out by Si the Spaniard, is that they memory-hole the former role of cash as a receipt for precious metals. "By getting rid of cash," he told the Red Pill Day conference in 2023, "they're getting rid of the last bit of evidence that they owe all this gold back to the people." CBDCs are also "the perfect mechanism for them to transact whatever money laundering they want, and no-one can really get to look at it."

Worse yet, if the parasite class can homogenize their digital tokens across nations, all the distinct national currencies will be collapsed into one currency to rule them all. This is another Tower of Babel. That Old-Testament building project was thwarted when the Almighty fractured the world's single language into various tongues, for it meant that the builders could no longer work together (*Genesis* 11:1-9), but now the 'globalists' seek to impose on Mankind one worldwide financial language.

You don't have to take my word for it. On Oct. 19, 2020, Augustin Carstens, the human toad heading the Bank for International Settlements, said, "A central bank will have absolute control under rules and regulations that will determine the use of that expression of central-bank liability, and also we will have the technology to enforce that."

If such a system of financial coercion is implemented, then medical coercion will intensify along with it, as Clayton Morris warns in a December 2023 episode of *Redacted News*:

> "You'll have no choice but to either get the vaccine, or we turn off your money supply. You'll not be able to go through a tollbooth, you'll not be able to get on an airplane, you'll not be able to go into this building, you won't be able to get on the subway because, when you scan your digital ID, 'Oh, you didn't get your vaccine, so we can't let you on the subway.' "

The implementation may require some "triggering event," according to former Pfizer executive and now whistleblower, Mike Yeadon. In March 2024, he told a meeting of Medical Doctors for COVID Ethics International that a financial crisis would be engineered to "destroy all sovereign currencies and steal all private wealth, then you'll have total dependency upon the state if you haven't got your own resources."

Even worse than the no-jab no-job decrees issued during COVID, the tyranny would expand to "No jab, no food; no jab, no money; no jab, no job; no jab, no travel. Your CBDC will simply not work." When you become a QR code, Yeadon adds, "You lose your humanity."

His answer? "We're not fucking taking digital ID. I would rather go to my grave as an analogue man than take digital ID."

So, when *Solari Report* founder Catherine Austin-Fitts calls CBDCs a "digital concentration camp," she's not exaggerating. Ultimately, they want to have us all carrying trackable devices under the skin, perhaps fulfilling end-time prophecy where a beast out of the Earth "forced everyone, small and great, rich and poor, free and slave, to receive a mark on his right hand or on his forehead, so that no-one could buy or sell unless he had the mark…" (*Revelation* 13:11-18).

This is the mad vision of 'globalists' such as Yuval Noah Harari, lizard sidekick to Klaus Schwab in the World Economic Forum, who said in October 2020,…

> "Maybe in a couple of decades, when people look back, the thing they will remember from the COVID crisis is, this is the moment when everything went digital, and this was the moment when everything became monitored, that we agreed to be [surveilled] all the time, not just in authoritarian regimes but even in democracies, and maybe most importantly of all, this was the moment when surveillance started going under the skin."

Harari even fantasized that such technology could have informed him he was gay before he discovered it for himself. Think of the possibilities. Just in case teachers haven't managed to persuade little children that they're gay or even trans, embedded AI technology could do it for them!

How, then, shall we prevent digital slavery? Our best hope is for mass non-compliance from a populace aware of the genocidal schemes in play. But then again, we may observe with dismay how many people went along with absurd COVID requirements and still go along with Constitution-crushing humiliation rituals at airports, how many fail to notice the sticky white trails in the sky above, how many buy listening devices to use in their own homes, and how many still look for a political saviour who will make all the bad stuff go away. We may even shudder to recall the bad things our fellow creatures wanted to do to us when we called into question government solutions to a purported emergency before.

And governments, of course, have a long track record of manufacturing emergencies, using them as a pretext to unleash violence, trample our Rights, and gin up fear to squelch dissent. It's how the U.S. feeds its war addiction, unleashes bioweapons on the People, and pursues its diabolical 'green' agenda.

The financial arena is as vulnerable to such tactics as any other. For example, in his Mar. 4, 1933 Inaugural Address during the 'Great Depression', then U.S. president Franklin D. Roosevelt declared the United States "a stricken nation in the midst of a stricken world" and called on Congress to grant him "broad Executive power to wage a war against the emergency, as great as the power that would be given to me if we were in fact invaded by a foreign foe."

Just two days later, he issued Proclamation 2039 announcing a four-day suspension of banking transactions. During that suspension, Congress passed the *Emergency Banking Act,* which FDR signed on Mar. 9, 1933. The Act effectively stripped gold backing from U.S. banknotes.

I looked at the Congressional Record surrounding this legislation and got a sense of the bewildered haste with which this rubber-stamp Congress did FDR's bidding, and of the flattery and deceit some House representatives exhibited. Among them was Congressman Martin Smith from Washington State, the epitome of a ring-kissing sycophant...

> "I shall vote for this measure, although I should like to have had an opportunity to study and consider its provisions. It has not been possible to do this, owing to the fact that the Bill has merely been read to us by the clerk this afternoon on the opening day of this special session without our being furnished copies thereof, and the Bill not being subject to amendment and only 40 minutes allowed for debate. This is a most extraordinary situation. However, we are advised by President Roosevelt in his message which has just been read, that the immediate passage of this legislation is absolutely necessary in order to reopen the banks in the nation and provide them with additional and adequate currency. We are further informed by our distinguished majority leader, Mr. Byrns, that the Senate is now awaiting the action of the House on this particular Bill, and that in order to reopen the banks of the country tomorrow, it must be enacted into law today. I shall therefore vote for the Bill, Mr. Speaker, because of these assurances of our great president and our able leaders in this body."
>
> — MAR. 9, 1933 — VOL. 77, PART 1, P.82

Next to chime in was Texas Congressman, John Patman...

> "The money will be worth 100 cents on the dollar, because it is backed by the credit of the nation. It will represent a mortgage on all the homes, and other property of all the people of the nation./ The money so issued will not have one penny of gold coverage behind it, because it is really not needed. We do not need gold to back our internal currency. We only need gold to settle our balances with foreign countries. Our people do not actually use gold as a medium of exchange; paper money is just as good and is much easier to handle" (p.83).

What a bone-headed assessment! Paper was paper, Patman was saying, whether it was backed by gold or not. But Minnesota representative Ernest Lundeen opposed, complaining, "we therefore have the spectacle of the great House of Representatives of the United States of America passing, after a 40-minute debate, a bill its Members never read and never saw, a bill whose author is unknown." The legislation, he warned, would further concentrate money and credit control in the hands of those already holding power.

> "I want to put myself on record against a procedure of this kind and against the use of such methods in passing legislation affecting millions of lives and billions of dollars... I am suspicious of this railroading of bills

> through our House of Representatives, and I refuse to vote for a measure unseen and unknown. I want the record to show that I was, and am, against this bill and this method of procedure; and I believe no good will come out of it for America."
>
> — MAR. 9, 1933 — VOL. 77, PART 1, P.83

Well, Representative Lundeen, you were right. No good did come out of it, and now, almost a century later, let the record show that you opposed it.

Within a month of railroading the *Emergency Banking Act,* FDR signed Executive Order 6102 on Apr. 5, 1933, requiring the People to surrender their gold by May 1 to the Federal Reserve.

POSTMASTER: PLEASE POST IN A CONSPICUOUS PLACE.—JAMES A. FARLEY, Postmaster General

UNDER EXECUTIVE ORDER OF THE PRESIDENT

issued April 5, 1933

all persons are required to deliver

ON OR BEFORE MAY 1, 1933

all GOLD COIN, GOLD BULLION, AND GOLD CERTIFICATES now owned by them to a Federal Reserve Bank, branch or agency, or to any member bank of the Federal Reserve System.

Executive Order

FORBIDDING THE HOARDING OF GOLD COIN, GOLD BULLION AND GOLD CERTIFICATES.

By virtue of the authority vested in me by Section 5(b) of the Act of October 6, 1917, as amended by Section 2 of the Act of March 9, 1933, entitled "An Act to provide relief in the existing national emergency in banking, and for

Section 4. Upon receipt of gold coin, gold bullion or gold certificates delivered to it in accordance with Sections 2 or 3, the Federal reserve bank or member bank will pay therefor an equivalent amount of any other form of coin or currency coined or issued under the laws of the United States.

Section 5. Member banks shall deliver all gold coin, gold bullion and gold certificates owned or received by them (other than as exempted under

This was a lordly scam. Those who complied were compensated at just $20.67 per troy ounce, but over the next year, as a Forbes article recounts, "the president then raised his official gold price to $35 per ounce." A nice earner for him, making the government a $2.8 billion windfall, but an appalling loss for the compliers who saw the value of their dollars fall by almost half in a year. It wasn't until 1974 that private ownership of gold coins, bars, and certificates was re-legalized by an Act of Congress signed by then president, Gerald Ford.

So, having marked down 1913 as a bad year for the States United (Sixteenth Amendment, income tax, *Federal Reserve Act*), we can do the same for 1933 with the *Emergency Banking Act,* bullion confiscation, and phenomenal currency devaluation.

Yet another milestone of financial tyranny came in 1971 when then president, Richard Nixon, took the U.S. off the gold standard entirely. This, according to Mike Maloney in Episode 9 of his *Hidden Secrets of Money* series, was "an unprecedented act of global debasement by a wanna-be emperor that would make any Roman ruler hang his head in shame."

We have been talking about the U.S. dollar, but the currencies of other nations are just as fraudulent. Britain too was gripped by a purported 'national emergency' in 1931 which led to rushed passage of the *Gold Standard Amendment Act,* a "temporary" measure to suspend the Gold Standard. That "temporary" measure is still in place today!

Nor is there safe haven in swapping one form of fiat currency for another. As financial consultant Jim Willie told *SGT Report* in a June 2024 interview, "All the major forex currencies are dollars with different jackets on, because they're all debt-based, upside-down, fiat, toilet-paper currency designed to fail."

I don't expect salvation from the emergent BRICS currency either. Though it is based on commodities, including gold, it is still a digital currency, and centrally controlled under the auspices of the Satanic Bank for International Settlements, sometimes called 'the central bank of central banks'. BRICS is therefore a convenient mechanism for world authorities to reward compliant behaviour and penalize dissent. It does not, to the best of my knowledge, have a cash version, but if you know different, or you have at some point held a 10-BRICS note in your hand, please let me know at the email address at the end of this book.

Meanwhile, there are yet more financial weapons aimed at us including bank failures, bank runs, and the ultimate horror of bank 'bail-ins' where they just help themselves to the contents of your account. There is precedent for this. *Solari Report*'s 2016 publication, *State of Our Currencies – Chronology* lists for Mar. 16, 2013:

> "In Cyprus, depositors drain cash from ATMs after European officials rule that part of a 10-billion-euro bailout must be paid for directly from the bank accounts of ordinary savers. An emergency deal in Brussels sets a levy of 9.9% on Cypriot bank deposits of more than 100,000 euros and 6.75% on less."

A bail-in scenario is also discussed in a Nov. 9, 2022

meeting of the U.S. Federal Deposit Insurance Corporation (FDIC) in a widely shared but since suppressed video clip. After all, our supposed 'deposit' with a bank is not really a deposit at all but an unsecured loan to the bank on which it may default at any time with impunity.

So, just in case our fellow creatures don't stand with us next time a crisis is concocted, what can we do to avoid the impoverishment and slavery planned for us? That is my theme in the next chapter.

5

SILVER LININGS

The Lord abhors dishonest scales but accurate weights are his delight.

— *PROVERBS* 11:1

You may find the idea of currency collapse alarming, but consider the liberation it may bring. When tyrants can no longer buy off politicians, spew propaganda, devise new weapons, fund wars, take over farmland, and construct diabolical infrastructure, all while poisoning our air, water, land, food, and bodies, then may our creative energies be renewed and released, and our endeavours find their due reward. When they can no longer get away with stealth taxation through fake currency production, we may suddenly find ourselves enjoying a level of prosperity unimaginable before.

Mike Adams is looking forward to this outcome too, saying in a Mar. 15, 2024 broadcast,...

> "The BRICS nations want to trade in things that are real. They want to buy and sell commodities, fertilizer, food, oil, energy, things that are real, things that actually drive economies, whereas the Western countries, they just want to pretend. They want to live in their fairytale land and pretend like everything's good, just print money and hope that that can last forever, which it won't, and they want to have fake news, fake elections, fake policies, fake science, fake medicine, fake pandemics, everything.
>
> That whole system is going to collapse, and thank God, by the way. Thank God it's going to collapse, and the fake currency will also collapse. So the collapse of the dollar is coming, and it can't happen fast enough as far as I'm concerned. The collapse of the dollar will be an event worth celebrating in terms of helping to set people free all over the world. Granted, there's going to be some short-term suffering. A lot of people will lose their life savings because they're gullible enough to believe in the dollar, believe in the government, believe in the Treasury."

The question is how we get through the transitional chaos that will follow financial implosion. To which I answer, look at how precious metals took centre stage following previous collapses. During the Great Depression, according to bullion trader Andrew Sleigh in an August 2024 interview with Dr Rima Laibow, "People bought city blocks for a couple of ounces of gold, and that is the ultimate way to realize the future value and gain in having metal. You got a house at that time for somewhere between 50 and 65 ounces of silver."

In terms of precious-metals prices at the time of writing (September 2024), that would mean buying a city block for about US$5100 and a house for less than $2000. In other words, gold and silver are super cheap now compared to their purchasing power in time of collapse. Sleigh calls them "the ultimate exit... when this whole system breaks. Everybody is broke except for the people sitting with metal, and your purchasing power of the metal is going to go through the roof on these other assets."

Silver

Further historical examples are provided by precious-metals analyst David Jensen in a May 2024 appearance on *SGT Report*. In ancient times, he noted, one-third of an ounce of silver bought a day's skilled labour. That would make an ounce of silver worth some $1500 today, Others assert that a day's skilled labour could be bought for just one-tenth of an ounce, making a silver ounce worth about $5000 today.

Either way, today's spot price of just over $30 is, again, super cheap. More recently, in Venezuela, a month's supply of food could be purchased for one ounce of silver. Jensen also points to the 2002 currency collapse in Argentina, after which food markets opened up in the streets and traded with individual links of gold necklaces.

So this raises the question about whether to hold gold or silver. Traditionally, gold is used for big-ticket items such as land, houses, and cars, and silver for more everyday items such as groceries and gas. If you don't have much cash to spare, then starting with silver is an easy entry point.

Silver is also historically cheap compared to gold. At the time of writing, an ounce of gold is trading at more than 85 times the price of an ounce of silver. If you take a look at the chart below, which tracks the ratio back to 1970, you will see this is close to the peaks around 100x that were briefly touched in 1991 and 2020.

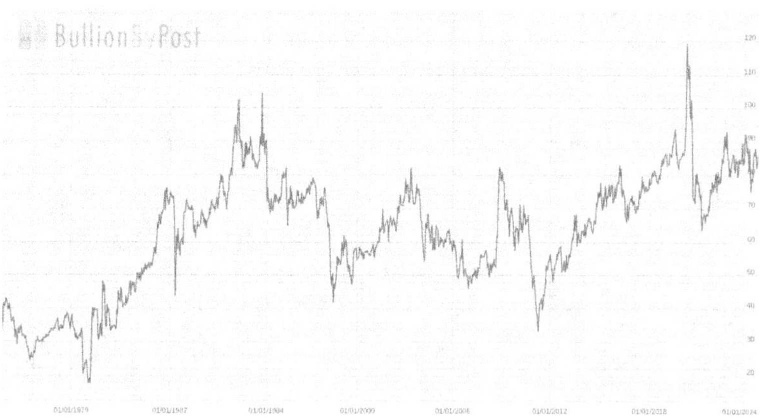

Now look at the ratio's historical low of around 15x at the close of 1979. If the gold-silver ratio went that low again for today's gold price, silver would now be around $170 per ounce. I have also heard that, in ancient Egypt, the ratio went as low as 2.5x, which would put silver at more than $1,000 per ounce today. Either way, today's $30 appears… super cheap!

TIME FRAME / ERA	Sell 1 oz Gold Bullion	To buy X oz of Silver
Menes, Egypt 3200 BC	1	2.5
Egypt, 2700 BC	1	9
Hammurabi, Mesopotamia 2700 BC	1	6
Egypt 1000 BC	1	10.0
Croesus, Lydia 550 BC	1	13.33
Persia under Darius, son of Hystaspes (father of Xerxes)	1	13.0
Plato, ca. 445 BC	1	12.0
Xenophon (in Persia)	1	11.66
Menander, ca. 341 BC	1	10.0
Greece, ca. 300 BC	1	10.0
Rome, 207 BC	1	14.5
Rome, 189 BC	1	10.0
Rome, 40 BC, Julius Caesar	1	7.5
Rome, Claudius	1	12.5
Constantine the Great	1	10.5

Gold/Silver ratio in ancient times. Source: SD Bullion

Now, add to that the observation of monetary historian Dave Silver, interviewed by Richard Vobes in

May 2024, that there is "a huge shortage of silver... This is the first time in history now that silver is more rare than gold in available supplies. It's never happened before." He also asserts silver mines are becoming depleted. Moreover, because silver is so widely used in electronics, telecoms, and solar panels, the tyrants could never hope to lock it all away beyond the reach of the People. Taking all this into account, holding silver seems a no-brainer.

Precious metals can be bought and held as bars or coins, and bars start as small as one gram. When I was living in England, I bought precious metal from bullionbypost.co.uk, and when in the States, from treasureislandcoins.com. (I don't have an affiliate arrangement with either.) American eagles are a popular coin for gold, the smallest unit being 1/10 troy ounce and about the size of a dime.

Having some cash on hand is also a good idea. Under *United States Code*, "United States coins and currency (including Federal reserve notes and circulating notes of Federal reserve banks and national banks) are legal tender for all debts, public charges, taxes, and dues" (Title 31, Section 5103).

Some say, "Cash is king." Well, it does give you Privacy in transactions and, in a scenario where banks are shuttered and ATMs no longer work, will give you some short-term purchasing power before the realization takes hold that it's worthless. But to call cash 'king' is ultimately absurd because it's just paper with various numbers printed on it. Rather, gold is king, silver is queen, and cash is an impoverished duke, but he's still better than CBDCs, which are a usurping tyrant.

Goldbacks

My favourite currency option, combining the supremacy of gold with the Privacy of cash, is the goldback, which came into being in 2019. Using novel technology, the goldback sandwiches a precise weight of 24-karat gold between two layers of polymer. The smallest denomination, a one goldback, contains 1/1000th of a troy ounce; the largest, a 50-goldback, contains 50/1000ths. The notes between are 5, 10, and 25.

They're beautiful to look at, and each has a unique serial number. Their market price tends to over-correlate to the price of gold, meaning that when the price of gold rises, goldbacks rise more. When the price of gold falls, goldbacks fall less. At the time of writing, goldbacks are trading at 5.27 U.S. dollars each, making the market price about double the spot price of the gold they contain. This makes sense, given the costs of production and design. When I began buying goldbacks in May 2023, the dollar price per goldback was about $3.70, meaning the value has increased by more than 40% in a little over a year.

You can also get a vertical wallet to keep your goldbacks so that you don't have to fold them. They are a good option for travel too. Though I have sometimes been questioned about silver bars in my hand luggage, my goldback wallet has never been flagged. If you're traveling with gold or silver coins, it makes sense to mix them in with a bag of regular change.

UPMA

If you want to buy goldbacks to hold, I do have a referral link at Geni.us/Goldbacks (no www). I also value the ability to vault goldbacks for free with the Utah-based United Precious Metals Association (UPMA) and to 'lease' some of them to gain interest. You can liquidate your vaulted goldbacks into U.S. dollars, have those dollars transferred to a regular bank account, and withdraw them at an ATM with a Truelink Visa card.

Another key benefit of this vaulting facility is that you can transfer goldbacks between UPMA members, and buy online from merchants. For example, one of my friends is a baker and fellow UPMA member. When I want to buy bread from her, I can simply transfer goldbacks online.

UPMA does not practice fractional-reserve banking. Its membership's holdings are 100% reserved in the vault, which is audited four times a year. My referral link if you want to join UPMA is Geni.us/UPMA (no www).

These innovations come at a time when legal

frameworks at the State level are becoming more friendly to precious metals. According to a May 2024 newsletter from Alpine Gold, the parent organization of UPMA, by then 23 States had recognized gold and silver as legal tender in physical or electronic form, with other States poised to follow.

In the same month, the U.S. House of Representatives passed the *CBDC Anti-Surveillance State Act* (H.R. 5403) which "halts unelected bureaucrats from issuing a central bank digital currency (CBDC)—which would threaten Americans' right to financial privacy—without explicit authorization from Congress." However, the legislation does not forbid CBDCs outright.

Bullion Buyer Beware

A note of caution is warranted, however, when buying other forms of bullion. Treasure Island Coins warned customers in an email, "There are a number of dealers in our industry who prey on uninformed Americans by selling bullion coins for 50%-100% above the actual precious metal value." The playbook includes: endorsement by celebrities and high-profile media figures; lack of transparent, live pricing on websites; no on-line purchasing, so that you have to call a salesman; and bait-and-switch tactics by which dealers try to lure you in with a good bullion deal, but pressure you to buy speculative, special-issue, or 'exclusive' coins instead.

Crypto

And what of cryptocurrencies? I dare say many of my readers have at least dabbled in them, and so have I, but my heart is not in it. My first objection is their complexity. When Christ told us his yoke is easy and his burden light, why are we dealing with such baffling concepts as 'blockchain', 'distributed ledger', 'proof-of-work', or 'proof-of-stake', and all of it to acquire something you cannot touch, feel, or see?

Intense surveillance is another problem. Bitcoin itself is massively corporatized and monitored, and the data collection before you can trade on crypto exchanges is brutal. As author and researcher Whitney Webb warned in a May 2024 interview with Jimmy Dore, "A lot of people have been talking about CBDCs—central-bank-issued digital currency—but there's also going to be digital currencies just as surveillable and programmable that are issued by the private sector and the Wall-Street banks, and that isn't being talked about enough."

So could Bitcoin be a trap? In July 2024, presidential candidate Donald Trump told a Bitcoin conference in Nashville, Tennessee that he wanted the United States to be "the crypto capital of the planet," and called Bitcoin "a miracle of human achievement." Well, he said similar about the "beautiful" vaccines he fathered, didn't he? But that didn't make it a good idea to take them.

I also heed the warning of Catherine Austin-Fitts, interviewed by James Delingpole in 2021, that crypto currencies are a ploy by the parasite class to have us buying digital assets so that we don't bid up the price of the real assets, such as land and natural resources, that they are quietly buying up for themselves in the meantime. Sneaky fuckers, huh?

Having said that, I take the point that no nation can counterfeit Bitcoin, so this property alone gives it utility. I was able to purchase some at a Bitcoin ATM in the States, and thereby avoid the extreme surveillance exacted by online crypto exchanges. You put in dollar bills and show the machine a QR code for your crypto 'wallet', so that it knows where to send the equivalent Bitcoin.

But after buying Bitcoin, it makes sense to swap at least some of it for 'privacy coins'. Monero is the most widely adopted privacy coin, while the qorts of Qortal and the pocketcoins of Bastyon appear to champion a freer financial future. Lode, at lode.one, is a crypto currency that tokenizes gold and silver that are held in audited vaults. Lode can be exchanged for physical delivery of the metal.

That's about all I have to offer on crypto. Others are far more adept and experienced in this, and they can take you further, but I am not convinced overall, certainly not when it comes to Bitcoin.

In Closing...

I should probably put a disclaimer somewhere in the book saying that I am not giving financial advice, to do your own research, that prices can rise and fall, etc. So consider that done. In any case, my primary purpose is not to maximize your investments but to minimize the cost of refusal when financial tyranny is attempted. Whether that means holding gold, silver, bars, coins, goldbacks, cash, or crypto is up to you, whether you hold or vault is up to you, and how you diversify among those assets, again, is up to you, but I trust you have heard the saying not to put all your eggs in one basket. In any case, we are learning new ways to embrace a freer financial future, and that is a godly endeavour if we are to "Come out of her, my people" (*Revelation* 18:4).

6

DEBT

"Slavery is now far worse than it ever was. They don't need chains, they just need debt... These are forms of slavery that just haven't got the taint of that name, but that is what they are."

— FRANCES LEADER, INTERVIEW WITH JAMES DELINGPOLE, MAY 2024

Strap yourself in. If you thought taxation was a fraud, behold the deceit of debt. I'm not talking about borrowing from a friend or family member, though that, as Polonius says in Shakespeare's *Hamlet* (I.iii), is inadvisable...

Neither a borrower nor a lender be
For loan oft loses both itself and friend,
And borrowing dulls the edge of husbandry.

But purported lending by financial institutions is an entirely different thing. David E. Robinson puts it succinctly in *Meet Your Strawman*: "The money does not come out of the bank's existing assets as the bank is simply inventing it, and in reality the bank is putting up nothing of its own, except for a fictional liability on paper."

Thus, as observed by John Titus, creator of the BestEvidence channel, "When I lend you a thousand dollars, I'm charging you interest because I don't have possession of that thousand dollars. That's not the case with commercial banks. The bank is charging you interest on something that did not exist to begin with. That is not interest. That is taxation."

These debt arrangements desecrate the basic principles of Contract. A Contract requires giving something in exchange for something else of commensurate value, or 'Equal Consideration'. If you have a loan agreement with a bank, you are agreeing to give the bank future payments, but the bank is giving you nothing; it is only adding digits to your bank balance at no cost to itself. That's why they'll tell you they are "advancing funds" to you but won't say they are "loaning money." They know they aren't; they just want you to infer that.

Also, a Contract must be entered into knowingly by both parties with 'Full Disclosure', but you did not knowingly enter it because you were not informed that the bank was risking nothing, and that its extra digits were conjured from your signature alone. Contracts also require wet-ink signatures of both parties, not photocopied ones or rubber stamps but, as Robinson points out, "Corporations can't sign because they have no Right or Mind to contract since they are soul-less legal fictions." In summary, he says,...

> "A loan agreement is a contract and so there has to be full disclosure of all the details (which there wasn't), both sides have to put up something of equal worth (which didn't happen), and the contract has to be signed in wet ink by both parties (which the bank can't do)."

Mortgages are no different. You gift the bank the fruit of your labour to supply it with multiples of the fake currency you think you borrowed, and you do so from what's left after the government has extracted 80% of what you generated. If you default, the bank will seize your property by invoking unlawful statutes, and may even seize some of your possessions too. As photographer and justice warrior Jonathan Dow told Richard Vobes in a February 2024 interview, "While you're repaying the mortgage, you're just basically giving money back that the bank never gave you in the first place."

And what is debt anyway, when it is enumerated in fiat currencies? Even if I nominally owed a quadrillion dollars, I would still owe nothing of substance. Then, if governments go to CBDCs, trying to swap out dollars or pounds or euros with some digital token, the fiction is exposed all the more. If you took out a loan in one of those currencies, then you were expected to pay instalments in that currency. The tyrants can't turn round and say, "Now you have to pay off your debt in fedcoin" or what have you, because that was never in your contract in the first place. The moment they do that, they confirm your debt is cancelled.

Even if they give their digital-only currency the same name as the prior paper currency and tell you they expect payment in the digital-only version, they are still in Breach of Contract because a currency that has been stripped of its paper component is a new currency, and you never agreed to make payments in a new currency.

Solutions

Meanwhile, what other solutions are at our disposal? Begin by observing whom your would-be extortioner is addressing. If it is an ALL-CAPS NAME, then it is not you. That PERSON is not known at your address. As Robinson notes in *Meet Your Strawman*, "The company invoicing the Strawman is hoping that you don't catch on to the fact that it is not you who is being billed."

Securitized debt?

It also helps to know if the bank has sold your supposed debt, i.e., 'securitized' it, turning it into a traded 'security'. This means some other institution has paid them a lump sum in order to take over receipt of your future instalments. The bank has effectively created a new counterparty for you without your permission. This is Breach of Contract and terminates the contract because you never agreed to make payments to that third party in the first place.

This is where Conditional-Acceptance strategies can come in, the rationale for which I discuss in *Know Your Lawful Rights*. By *conditionally* accepting the demands of corporate extortioners, rather than outright refusing, you are keeping things out of court because there is no controversy to trigger court involvement. And staying out of court is generally a good thing because the legal system is essentially an enforcement tool of the banking system. Even the word 'bench', where a judge sits, has the same origin as the word 'bank'.

Robinson suggests,...

> "If a company starts demanding payment of large sums of money, you start by asking them to provide the 'accounting' for the deal. In other words, you are asking them to show in writing that they provided something of genuine worth as their side of the loan contract. As they invented the money as numbers in their books, with no real worth attached to those numbers, they are in deep trouble as they can't comply with your demand."

This approach is fortified by writing to the purported lender,...

" 'First, there is a need to verify the debt, so please send me a bill with a human signature on it. Also, I need to see the lawful, two-party contract supporting that bill.'

"As they can't supply either of those things, it kills the claim stone dead, so just keep insisting that they either supply those things or else stop bothering you."

He imagines the hypothetical case of a James Martin who has received a loan from Swindle Bank Inc...

"The bank will probably send a Statement of what it wants James to believe is the outstanding amount. James should return this with a polite note saying that a 'Statement' is not an 'Invoice', so would they please provide a signed 'Invoice' as requested. They will also probably send a photocopy of his Loan Application form, at which point James should write back and point out politely that it does not constitute a contract as it is only signed by one of the parties (himself) and he has asked for a copy of the Contract signed by both parties.

"The bank is likely to go silent at this point and stop corresponding with James. James should then write again, requesting that the necessary documents be sent to him within the next fourteen (or perhaps 28) days, and if that does not happen, then he will consider the [alleged] debt to be fully discharged.

"The bank will either remain silent or write back to say that the debt is fully discharged. If the bank tries phoning, then just tell them politely that you only wish to deal with this matter in writing, and hang up. If the

> bank remains silent for the stated period of time, then James should write back stating that, due to the bank's failure to provide the necessary evidence of a lawful debt within the reasonable period of time provided, that James now considers that the [alleged] debt is fully discharged, and ask the bank to confirm that in writing. The bank will normally write back confirming that the debt is fully discharged and that there is nothing owing, and if it does not do that, it will just stop asking for any further payments."

Another Conditional-Acceptance strategy comes from Si the Spaniard, speaking at a Bournemouth conference in January 2023,...

> "You play a game. You play a game where you're using your knowledge of the fact that there is no loan. There never was. And so you offer to buy back the credit agreement, because in 97% of cases, they've sold that credit agreement, they don't have it. So what you do is, you offer to buy it... They sold it, which means it's already been paid off. The point is, they can't give it back to you. So when you're going to discharge a debt, or you want to wipe a debt off, what do you do? You offer to discharge it on condition they return the instrument to you, which you know they cannot do."

If a debt collector comes to your door, ask who they are working for. Is it for the original financial institution, or is it for some debt-collection company that has bought the alleged debt? If the latter, then the collection company has effectively paid *off* the debt! Tell them to provide Proof of any debt and a signed Contract with *them*, not the original 'lender', proving that you agreed to pay it to that collection company.

Also require a contract between them and the original creditor authorizing them to collect, including disclosure of any commission they will receive if they succeed. If they call, tell them to send any communications in writing because you will not discuss anything over the phone.

A 'Notice' is just an offer.

Bear in mind, too, that a 'Notice' is not a bill or an invoice. I have seen notices affixed to lamp posts, and on notice boards in shops, theatres, cinemas, clubs, churches, factories, schools, universities, hospitals, clinics, libraries, and in public parks. I have seen them scrawled on toilet walls, but none may compel me.

Robinson writes,...

> "All men are born equal and so nobody has the right to command you, make demands of you, or force you to do anything. The most that anyone can do is to make you an offer to perform./ Even though they may say that it is an 'Order' or a 'Demand' or a 'Summons', it is in reality an offer which you are free to accept or not as you so choose."

He is echoed by Allegedly Dave who, in a 2023 conversation with Richard Vobes, likens the corporate/government/banking extortion process to a set of railway tracks that culminate in payment or punishment. "The trick is to not let them put you on those tracks." If you receive a 'Notice' in the post, it really means in Legal speak that they've sent you an Offer. "At that point, you're not on the tracks yet; they're making you an Offer... but there are ways of holding them at the Offer stage."

If things go to court, @Funnyfresh561 on TikTok advises asking the judge if anyone on the claimant/plaintiff side is required to have first-hand knowledge of the case. The answer has to be yes, otherwise any evidence or testimony brought against you is hearsay. Having a photocopy of a contract is not first-hand knowledge! Then request the court to ask the opposing party who among them has any first-hand knowledge. Chances are they are empty-handed.

Mortgages and 'Promissory Notes'.

When it comes to mortgages, the fraud goes especially deep. As Allegedly Dave told Vobes in another interview, when you sign a mortgage agreement, you create a 'Promissory Note' which has value as currency. After all, If a central bank can conjure currency out of thin air by putting numbers on a piece of paper and a meaningless "Promise to pay the Bearer on Demand," why shouldn't you or I?

If you take a look at Bank of England bank notes over time, you will see how even this empty promise has been rendered in shrinking fonts, so that now you need a magnifying glass to read it. The word 'pound', when it describes the currency, originates from 8th-century Anglo-Saxon England when a pound of currency meant one pound in weight of silver, equivalent to 240 silver pennies. You would need hundreds of pounds in currency today to buy one pound weight of silver, especially after you add tax, retailer premiums, and delivery costs.

When you write your Promissory Note, you effectively increase the national currency supply. Now, you might think it silly that you or I could put numbers on a piece of paper and call it currency, but the *Bills of Exchange Act* (1882)—which is mirrored by similar Acts in other countries—says we can because, according to Allegedly Dave, the Act equates a Promissory Note to cash.

I did not find the word "cash" in the Act, but Dave also quotes a 1969 court ruling in Fielding & Platt Ltd. v. Selim Najjar where then Master of the Rolls, Tom Denning, stated, "We have repeatedly said in this court that a bill of exchange or a Promissory Note is to be treated as cash."

I haven't located the original court document, but your mortgage lender takes the idea seriously. Dave explains, "They take the Promissory Note that you create when you sign that mortgage agreement, and then they sell it without you knowing... on the securities market." This means that, if you are ever in legal action against the bank, they won't be able to produce their Contract with you.

So we have at least three official confirmations that, yes, you and I can write cash into existence with a Promissory Note: the *Bills of Exchange Act*, the Denning statement, and the fact that mortgage lenders themselves treat them as cash.

Knowing this, let's review the multiple payments banks receive through the mortgage game: not just your hard-earned interest payments on the empty digits they added to your bank balance, which will amount to multiples of the original principal, but also the value of your Promissory Note, which the bank will typically sell in the securities market.

Then, if you 'default' on your mortgage, the bank doesn't mind a bit because it still gets paid from insurance it takes out against defaults. Now, the bank gets to evict the home-buyer and take over the asset, which it can then sell to someone else.

Dave has calculated that, for every £100,000 of principal in mortgage loans, banks make £1.8 million, whether you 'pay it back' or not! As Vobes comments, "No wonder they want to keep on building houses… It's a bloody fraud, and you've been taken for a ride all along."

Dave is a developing a 'Mortgage Project' to turn the tables on the banks with a Promissory-Note strategy. He is creating "an instrument that they can't resist" and invites those who want to get rid of mortgage debt to email him at dmurphy25@gmail.com.

One famous story with Promissory Notes comes from South African author and activist, Michael Tellinger. In a video recorded in 2014, he explains how he used four Promissory Notes to pay Standard Bank in South Africa some 800,000 rand. His template (at https://www.michaeltellinger.com/promissory-notes/) uses legally precise wording and can be adapted for your country.

In the example below, Tellinger has promised to pay monthly instalments of 500 rand but specified that the bank will need to come to his address to collect the payments. Then, knowing that the bank will sell this instrument, he has wisely added that, once the recipient is using it in financial trade—in other words, the Promissory Note is being used as a 'Negotiable Instrument—"such trade shall terminate the obligation herein."

Once the bank fails to collect its first payment, Tellinger assumes it is trading with his Promissory Note, ending his obligation. Beneath the video, he has posted detailed instructions, including the proviso that this is only to be used to pay banks and government departments, not people or ordinary businesses.

Essentially, all you need for a Promissory Note is to write an amount in numbers, the same amount in words, and a signature, as Dave Silver told Vobes in their May 2024 conversation. One strategy to deal with debt collectors is to write them a Promissory Note for the amount they are demanding, less five pounds. You then write your Note on a piece of paper, staple a five-pound note to it, laminate the whole thing if you can, and present that as your full payment.

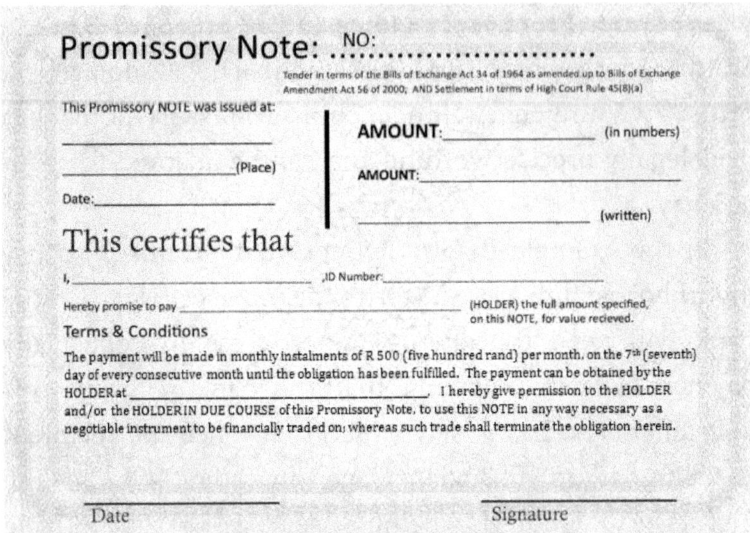

Promissory Note: NO: ....

Tender in terms of the Bills of Exchange Act 34 of 1964 as amended up to Bills of Exchange Amendment Act 56 of 2000; AND Settlement in terms of High Court Rule 45(8)(a)

This Promissory NOTE was issued at:

____

________________________(Place)

Date:____________________

AMOUNT:________________ (in numbers)

AMOUNT:________________________

________________________ (written)

This certifies that

I,______________________________ ,ID Number:______________________

Hereby promise to pay ______________________________ (HOLDER) the full amount specified, on this NOTE, for value recieved.

Terms & Conditions

The payment will be made in monthly instalments of R 500 (five hundred rand) per month, on the 7th (seventh) day of every consecutive month until the obligation has been fulfilled. The payment can be obtained by the HOLDER at ______________________________. I hereby give permission to the HOLDER and/or the HOLDER IN DUE COURSE of this Promissory Note, to use this NOTE in any way necessary as a negotiable instrument to be financially traded on; whereas such trade shall terminate the obligation herein.

________________ Date

________________ Signature

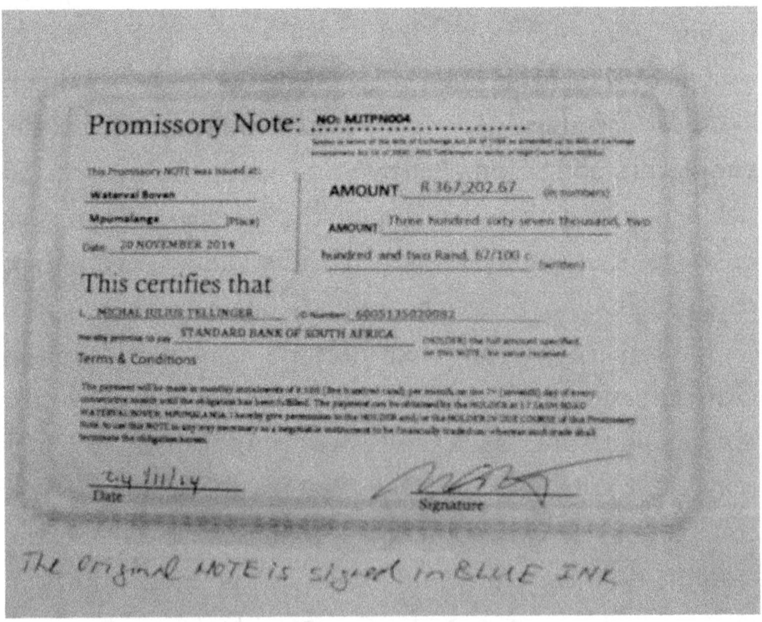

Promissory Note: NO: MJTPN004

Waterval Boven

Mpumalanga (Place)

Date: 20 NOVEMBER 2014

AMOUNT R 367,202.67

AMOUNT Three hundred sixty seven thousand, two hundred and two Rand, 67/100 c

This certifies that

I, MICHAL JULIUS TELLINGER

Hereby promise to pay STANDARD BANK OF SOUTH AFRICA

Terms & Conditions

24/11/14 Date

Signature

The Original NOTE is signed in BLUE INK

According to Allegedly Dave, banks are reluctant to refuse Promissory Notes because that would mean taking you to court, which would expose their game. And if they don't return Promissory Notes, it suggests they value them as a source of income.

Paying from the 'Cestui Que Vie Trust'.

Yet another way to deal with bills is to use the 'Cestui Que Vie Trust', an approach championed by Australian, Mike Holt, of Citizens Initiated Referendums (CIR) (at cirnow.com.au). (I dislike this use of the word 'citizen', of course. I also oppose calling legislation "law," which he and the CIR website do. Still, as they say in 12-Step groups, "Take what you want and leave the rest behind.")

First, let's do a quick review of the English *Cestui Que Vie Act* of 1666, which I looked at in *Know Your Lawful Rights*. Its title in archaic French, which was the dominant language used for legal documents in England at the time, means something like, "Whoever Is Alive." Spanning just two pages, the Act addresses what to do about the estates of missing persons "beyond the Seas or absenting themselves," and it determines that the missing person "shall be accounted as naturally dead" after seven years of absence if there is no proof that he is alive. Then his property would be handed over to a 'Reversioner', meaning the one to whom the property reverts, the one in line to receive it after his death.

This Act has been misapplied to us. We are deemed missing "beyond the Seas" and therefore legally dead, so each of us has been assigned an ALL-CAPS NAME such as that engraved on a tombstone. When we reached the age of seven, the banking cabal, which has somehow set itself up as 'Reversioner', took over our estates. Allegedly Dave explains, in a September 2024 interview with James Delingpole, "They've used this idea of everyone's dead to claim our shares of the country."

But the *Cestui Que Vie Act* also says that if the supposed dead man shall "returne againe from beyond the Seas" or prove to be alive, then he "may reenter repossesse have hold and enjoy" his property again. Furthermore, he may recover the revenues withheld from him, with interest, from the time the Reversioner took over his property.

So what happens between the date we were deemed legally dead and our coming declaration that we are really alive and ready to take up our rightful inheritance? This is where Trusts come in because those awfully nice banker types have been holding our Estates in Trust, hoping of course that we won't find out and that the day of our return shall never come.

So let's also do a quick review of Trusts, again distilling my analysis from *Know Your Lawful Rights*. A simple Trust has three parties, and can be illustrated using Charles Dickens' novel, *Great Expectations*. The protagonist, Pip, discovers he is the Beneficiary of a Trust that shall fund his transformation from a blacksmith's apprentice to a 'gentleman'. The Trust is administered by the lawyer, Jaggers, who is entrusted with parcelling out the benefit.

Jaggers, therefore, is the Trustee, but he is not

permitted to tell Pip who granted the Trust into existence in the first place—that is to say, who the Grantor, Settlor, Donor, or Trustor is. As that anonymity is a key plot point, I won't spoil it here.

When it comes to the Cestui Que Vie Trust, each of us has $100s of millions, according to the CIR website, but it has been "hidden from us by CEOs, Banks, Insurance Companies, Government, ATO, Courts, Federal Reserve etc., all of whom know the truth." So, Brothers and Sisters, we have a life-changing amount of property and back-pay due to us, and under the tyrants' own legal structure, our announcement that we are alive entitles us to repossess it.

Does this explain government actions in recent years? If millions of us got wind of our Cestui Que Vie entitlement, tracked down the Trustee, and declared ourselves to be alive and therefore the Beneficiary, the cabal would be overwhelmed and exposed. Rather than face this calamity, they could either inflate the currency into oblivion so that the payouts became meaningless, or vastly reduce the number of people in a position to say they are alive, or both.

In any case, we can still dip into the Cestui Que Vie Trust now to pay off any tax bill, utility bill, or bank debt addressed to the ALL-CAPS NAME because the ALL-CAPS NAME is the Title Holder of the Trust.

So how does it work? Back in the day when I was paid wages with slips of paper called 'cheques', the payer would write or print my name on the paper, followed by the sum to be paid, expressed both as numbers and again in words. They would sign it, date it, and give it to me, then I would take it to my bank and sign the back of it, called 'endorsing' the cheque.

Then I would hand the cheque to the bank teller who would pay it into my account, or give me the equivalent cash. The cheque would then work its way through 'clearing' until it removed the same sum from the payer's bank account.

Talking to Richard Vobes in January 2024, Holt explained that when you receive a bill from 'GovCorp', such as a Fine, Penalty Notice, Utilities Bill, Loan Statement, or Mortgage Statement, the format looks like a cheque because that's what it is, "a cheque drawn on your Cestui Que Vie Trust." Above the ALL-CAPS NAME on the bill is a bar code which, Holt claims, is "the access to your Cestui Que Trust bank account."

If, then, you use your private funds to 'pay the bill', you have effectively paid twice. So, instead of doing that, you endorse the cheque by signing it. Then, Holt continues, the GovCorp entity uses that information to get the funds from your Cestui Que Vie Trust. That endorsement could take the form shown on the CIR website, which I now reproduce with slight adjustments. Write on the bill IN BLUE INK...

> THIS BILL/ OFFER IS ACCEPTED AS CASH FOR THE [DOLLAR/POUND/EURO] AMOUNT SHOWN HERE.
>
> [Draw an arrow to the Amount Due]

NOW, TAKE IT BACK AND USE IT AS REMITTANCE AND SETTLE THE ACCOUNTS.

Yours Honourably

[Your Name]

Named Estate Trust Title Holder (not the Trustee)

[Your Signature]

[Date]

Without Prejudice

Your endorsed cheque is now a 'Bill of Exchange', in legal parlance, and legal tender. Holt attests the GovCorp entity cannot refuse it because they are legally obliged to accept it under a *Bills of Exchange Act*.

I have mentioned the *U.K. Bills of Exchange Act* (1882) before, but all countries that have signed up to the *Uniform Commercial Code* (*UCC*) have their own version of it, according to Holt, and "if your country has a central bank, it comes under *UCC* rules." Several such Acts are linked at the CIR website, including Australia's, passed in 1909, and Norway's, passed in 1932. For the U.S., the equivalent legislation is *UCC* Title 3.

The U.K. version of the Act states that a Bill of Exchange "is dishonoured by non-acceptance" (43(1)), after which "no presentment for payment is necessary"

(43(2)). Similarly, *UCC* states that if tender of payment is refused, the endorser's obligation is discharged (Title 3, Section 603(b)). In other words, the alleged debt is paid by your endorsed cheque, whether the GovCorp entity likes it or not.

vicroads

Registration renewal

Your vehicle will be unregistered if you fail to pay by the due date.

Registration no.	
Vehicle type	Mazda Sedan
Amount due	$864.40
Due date	08 Dec 2022

Fee breakdown	Amount
Registration fee	$312.20
TAC charge*	$502.00
Insurance duty	$50.20
Total due	$864.40

Add a concession

Set and forget

Moving house?

Don't have a myVicRoads account yet?

Choose new, shorter rego period

How to pay

BPay

Biller Code: 216291

Reference number: 5281 4105 9225 688

Pay online

Australia Post

Payment code:

AKP683 A 08 Dec 2023 05822568 86440

Call us

Call 1300 086 314 to pay over the phone with Mastercard or VISA. A surcharge applies for all card payments.

Direct debit

Sign up to myVicRoads to set up direct debit payments. For all other payment channels visit vicroads.vic.gov.au

Once a GovCorp entity receives your endorsed cheque, it can take it to a bank, along with all its other conventional cheques, and the bank will accept it as cash. Holt attests that this method has been used to settle large tax bills. In case the GovCorp entity resists, you can find templates for your follow-up letters at lipforms.com. You can email Holt himself at mike@mikeholtshow.com or mikeh@commonlaw.earth.

Though I question why you would give tyrant bankers, whose proclivity is to squander and steal, permission to take *anything* from your Trust Fund to pay their unlawful bills, I admit there is elegance and simplicity in the method. You regard any GovCorp bill you receive as a cheque awaiting your endorsement and treat it as such. You still get to limit the amount they can take, and it's a drop in the bucket compared to what you have in there. So it's up to you.

Utility Bills

Vobes himself used this endorsed-cheque method to pay a utility bill. When he received the next bill, he saw that the previous amount had been credited to him, but after he went public about this, the utility company refused to accept this method the next time. Still, they didn't send the document back to him, suggesting it is valuable to them. At the time of publication, Vobes is pressing on with his quest.

Your own meter?

But why pay at all? Kayles, founder of the Telegram group Free Energy Nationwide, told Vobes in their November 2023 conversation that "utility bills are already pre-paid through our income taxes" and that so-called 'suppliers' are just middlemen operating as brokers between you and the National Grid. They only rent the serial numbers on energy meters in homes, but they don't own them, nor do they own any of the other infrastructure.

Members of Kayles' Telegram group hire a qualified engineer from her team to replace their meters or 'smart' meters (which communicate directly with a utility 'supplier'). The engineers install new and non-smart meters that are not attached to any database shared by the energy-broker network. "You're removing the meter that's in the property because you don't want to use a meter that the brokers have on their database."

For health reasons alone, it is essential to remove 'smart' meters from your dwelling because they emit harmful radiation. And don't fall for a supplier's/broker's claim that they have switched your smart meter to 'dumb mode'.

Once you have replaced your meter, "you have your own meter that you own," Kayles explains. You're not bypassing metering, but now, "You gain energy in exactly the same way as you did before; you just don't have to send meter readings anywhere." Then, you may want to get a safety certification done on your property. This will thwart any attempt by the corporate predators to force their way into your home on the pretext of safety concerns.

Meanwhile, you close your account with the broker. There are various ways to do this. As Kayles points out, you never had a valid contract with them in the first place, no Offer, no Agreement, and no wet-ink signature on either side.

The simplest procedure is to give final meter readings to the broker and close your account. You may choose to pay their final bill or not, depending on your situation. Ignore any subsequent letters addressed to 'THE OCCUPIER' or 'THE OWNER'. That's not you.

Of course, the powers-that-shouldn't-be don't like any of this and will try to make an example of a few, including what Kayles calls 'pantomime visits', where they show up with a purported Warrant to force-fit a prepayment meter. The Warrant, however, is typed up in a purely administrative procedure that omits any wet-ink signature from a judge. She continues,...

> "Every Warrant of Entry that I've seen in the last two years—and I've seen a lot—they're all the same, they're electronic, they're printed off or on little iPads. They don't tend to give you a copy because they don't want you to have them because they know they're invalid."

The Warrants aren't even addressed to the legal fiction of the ALL-CAPS NAME but to 'THE OCCUPIER'. They also purport to allow the 'operator' to enter your house but, as Kayles points out, the real operator is National Grid which doesn't send people round to your house, nor does it need to because it has already been paid. The 'suppliers'/brokers are billing agents, not operators.

The supporting cast of these pantomime teams may include an engineer and a locksmith who have forgotten they are personally liable if they proceed without checking the validity of any Warrant they are acting under. Just in case, you may want to add a solid bolting mechanism to the inside of your front door, along with other security precautions and, if you have an outside meter, change the lock on its casing. More information, documentation, and support are available on the Telegram group, Free Energy Nationwide, and I will have more to say about thwarting unwelcome visitors in the next chapter.

National Debt

Now, what of so-called 'national debt', and those debt 'clocks' with astronomically large numbers increasing at astronomical speeds? Is national debt really a thing? When currency is meaningless paper or digits, and will eventually be useless anyway, any debt enumerated in the currency is also zero. It's 'a fiction designed to enslave us and all future generations to paying off a fictional thing.

Seems to me debt clocks are a psychological operation designed to make you feel chained to a lifetime of servitude, but you and I signed no contract agreeing to take on this purported liability. National debt, if it exists, is what one corporation owes to another; it has nothing to do with us. And if it has been run up by politicians and bureaucrats, let them be the ones to pay it!

In Closing…

Imagine what prosperity would reign without the curse of debt, mortgages, bankruptcies, debt-collectors, repossessions, and so on. Of course, the banking cabal won't relinquish their power and control easily, but I trust this chapter has helped to fortify you for the battles ahead as we restore our Rights and Birthright. It boils down to this: If they want to allege a debt, they have to prove it, and they can't.

7

CONFISCATION

> The mugger points a gun at your face and says, 'Your money or your life!', but the government says, 'We'll take both!'
>
> — MIKE ADAMS, BROADCAST OF MAY 22, 2024

You've likely heard the World Economic Forum's diabolical slogan, "You will own nothing, and be happy." It originated in 2016 but became widely quoted during the COVID years. The idea is hardly new, however, even in the West. In 1933, the U.S. Senate published a paper titled *Contracts Payable in Gold* that declared, "The ultimate control of all property is in the State; individual so-called 'ownership' is only by virtue of Government." The individual, it argued, was a "mere user," and use must be "subordinate to the necessities of the State" (Document No. 43 , 73rd Congress, 1st Session, p.13). Like I said, 1933 was a bad year for the States United.

Since then, the banking vampires have gone a long way to achieving their goal of universal dispossession through taxation, inflation, and debt but, to fully strip the People of the little they have left, confiscation is the final solution. Their ploys include whipping up climate-change fears in order to impose measures so costly and onerous that owners are forced to give up their property.

Their schemes will fail eventually, but before I describe how we turn the tables on them, let us address this Biblically first. Many prophecies spring to mind, but *Job* 27 will do for now to describe what shall befall the wicked...

> *Though he heaps up silver like dust*
> *and clothes like piles of clay,*
> *what he lays up, the righteous will wear,*
> *and the innocent will divide his silver...*
> *He lies down wealthy, but will do so no more;*
> *when he opens his eyes all is gone.*

A massive downward transfer of wealth is coming which will suddenly reverse the centuries of theft perpetrated against us, and it will take the tyrants by surprise. In the meantime, let us stand our ground, and stand with the likes of Jim Gale, founder of Food Forest Abundance. He didn't ask for government approvals to create his oasis of effortless food production at Galt's

Landing near Orlando, Florida. In a March 2024 interview, he told Mike Adams,...

> "We've now built 11 structures here, and we did not ask, nor will we ever ask, the slave-masters for permission... and we are saying 'No', we will not only not comply, but we will demonstrate a better way, and we will invite you to do the better way with us, but we're not going to do it your way."

If you haven't figured it out by now, governments and their puppet-masters want to starve, impoverish, deaden, and destroy "all that is true, all that is holy, all that is just, all that is pure, all that is lovely, and all that is worthy of praise..." (*Philippians* 4:8). That includes independent food production. Thus, they will invent or inflate disease scares to cull entire flocks of birds, herds of livestock, and colonies of bees, and they will call 'good' their evil agenda to bring sickness, famine, and despair on the People.

In *Know Your Lawful Rights,* I pointed out how the British government is telling everyone who has even a single chicken to register their birds, but they will call you the 'keeper', not the 'owner', of your flock. Remember that, whenever you register something, you are giving it away to the entity you are registering it with. After the British government issued its decree, *Farmers Weekly* dutifully echoed it with a short article that used the word 'keeper' eight times, but never the word 'owner'!

The state owns your car, too, and you get to rent it through registration and licencing fees. And even the Certificate of Title on your house is not the Title itself but an official document that certifies a Title exists. You do not have 'Allodial' Title, which would make you king of your land.

Even if you've fully paid off your mortgage, you still don't own your house, according to the bankers. They may call you 'Proprietor' instead, which is not the same thing or, as campaigner Peter Wilson told Richard Vobes in an April 2024 interview, 'Tenant'...

> "Anybody that owns the house can go and check now. Get your Deeds, get them out, have a look at it, and it'll tell you point blank in black and white you are the tenant if you've paid your mortgage off, or even if you were lucky enough to actually have enough cash to buy that house outright—you've paid it off, you do not owe a penny—you are a tenant, that's all you are, a tenant on the land. You do not own it because it's all owned by the Crown. Therefore, it's all held in trust for them, but you can only be a tenant on the land."

A similar analysis is given by retired doctor K.L. in a May 2024 interview with *SGT Report*. "Your home, your car, everything is a publicly registered property. Your name is publicly registered when your birth is registered. So you're considered booty of war, along with the homes, along with all of the cars." The States United, he contends, have been under military occupation since

1933, a status confirmed by the use of gold-fringed flags in courtrooms. "You might as well think of them as military tribunals," he added.

Even your stocks and bonds are up for grabs according to David Rogers Webb, author of *The Great Taking*, who told Economic War Room (Episode 288) that you are legally severed from property rights in the case of securities and that you are essentially "an unsecured creditor to get your own securities back in the event of bankruptcy in the financial system... You have a claim but it's a weak claim in the event of insolvency."

Thus, the bankers have crafted a system that permits them to take risky bets and to win huge if the bet goes their way, but if the bet goes against them and they lose huge, your assets are their collateral. This has been going on since at least 1934, according to author Anna von Reitz in a June 2022 presentation. "Part of the evil was that they seized upon our gold and silver to pay their debts," she said. In 1934, the corporation calling itself the UNITED STATES OF AMERICA, INCORPORATED issued gold-bearer bonds against the People's gold, which was taken to the Philippines and placed in 'safe-keeping'.

They're after your intangible property too, your hopes and dreams. As an author trying to get out works true and edifying, I can attest to the dispiriting weight of bans and censorship and demonetization that are calculated not just to deprive readers of key information but to discourage creators and truth-tellers too.

Surely, all of this is illegal, you might say. Well, that depends on which legislation you're citing, for most legislation is an abomination, hateful in the eyes of Man and God, blasphemous to the Creator in whose image we are made. However, the Supreme Court of North Carolina spoke truth in its Hoke vs. Henderson decision of 1833, saying that when legislators "pass an act upon a subject upon which the people have said in the Constitution, they shall not legislate at all." The 'color-of-law' statutes in the *United States Code* also embody this principle.

Trusts

So what can we do? According to Si the Spaniard in a July 2019 presentation, Trusts can act as a "protective shield" that "ring-fence" your assets. As a Trustee doesn't hold 'Absolute Title' to a property in a Trust, and therefore cannot be said to own it, debt collectors cannot come after him. Nor can they come after the Beneficiary, because he doesn't hold Absolute Title either. He only holds Beneficial Title. Si continues,...

> "The property, for all intents and purposes, is kind of floating out there in the ether in terms of ownership. So it's very difficult to pin down who owns this property. Plus, of course, the Trustee is under no obligation to divulge who the Beneficiary is—in other words, who's entitled to this property. So what you have is a situation where property can be kind of shielded or masked, hidden in a kind of invisibility cloak."

By putting your assets into Trust, Peter Wilson

explained to Vobes in their April 2024 conversation, you remove them from the 'estate' of your ALL-CAPS NAME because the government cannot go after assets outside of that estate. You're basically saying to them, " 'You can't have something that's not mine.' "

A Trust contract is agreed between a Grantor and a Trustee, wherein the Grantor conveys legal title to a property into a Trust. The Trustee, who could be a reliable friend or family member, agrees to fulfil the specified duties and responsibilities of the Trust for the benefit of the Beneficiary. That Beneficiary could be you because you're the one who will travel in the car or live in the house.

Then, if you are ever the subject of bankruptcy proceedings, and a receiver asks why you have not listed your house or car among your assets, Wilson advises telling them, "That's in a Trust. It does not form part of my estate." He attests that this approach has a proven track record. It is also effective, he says, in thwarting local councils when they want to put your aging parent in a care facility and liquidate your family home to pay the exorbitant care-home fees.

Making a Trust, Wilson asserts, is not as daunting as it sounds. "All Trusts are just paperwork," he told Vobes. "You're doing it on a non-statutory basis, so you're not relying on any Acts or governments or parliaments or anything to do that."

As with every other approach I discuss in this book series, my preference is always to draw up my own documents and never to involve lawyers. If you pay someone to draw up a Trust for you, more caution may be warranted. Si the Spaniard argues the *Legal Services Act* (2007) deems paid Trust creation an activity 'reserved' to regulated practitioners such as barristers, notaries, or solicitors. Wilson, on the other hand, says lawyers betray your Privacy by registering your Trust with the false taxation authorities.

Collectors

But what if the thieves of Officialdom show up on your doorstep? I will focus especially on the U.K., but the analysis will be similar in your country. If a stranger comes to your door demanding payments or declaring their intention to seize your property, you wouldn't hesitate to send them away empty-handed, perhaps with a flea in their ear or even a "bloody good hiding" to reinforce the message. But somehow, the situation is perceived differently when uniforms, lanyards, and clipboards are involved. These are the props and costumes of the Theatre of the Legal, and they are trying to fool you into thinking you are in the same play.

As Vobes observes in a splendid rant about enforcement officers, "you've got to have no morals whatsoever, no ethics, of course, and bang on people's doors early in the morning, any old time, and demand money with menaces." Debt collectors go after the most vulnerable people, he continues, and give no Due Process to those they target, "and you don't need any paperwork, just bluff, just bluff your way through... and they're very threatening, and if you don't pay, the police turn up and end up aiding and abetting."

Thwarting Trespass.

The first line of defence, even before uninvited corporate intruders show up, is to put a notice on your front door or gate saying, "PRIVATE — BY APPOINTMENT ONLY." Such a notice is legally equivalent to a closed door, and it forbids a bailiff to enter your garden or driveway. It also gives you something to point to when you ask if they can read. You let it be known that you only see people by appointment, and they will need to contact you to agree a date and time. You will also let them know what you charge for your time if they want to take some of it.

Make sure to identify them too. Under *Criminal Procedure Rules* (2013), agents claiming court authority to seize property must, on request, show a written statement including their name, who they are working for, and Proof that they are authorised to execute Warrants (Rule 52.8). So have them spell out their name and their employer's name and demand their office phone number, and write down the information. Also, under the *Tribunals Courts and Enforcement Act (2007)*, "A person is guilty of an offence if, knowingly or recklessly, he purports to act as an enforcement agent without being authorised to do so..." (Section 63(6)).

A ploy often used by extortioners is to claim they are employed by a court when they are really working for a private company. If they make that claim, tell them to provide their court registration number. If they can't do that, they are guilty of 'fraud by false representation' under the *Fraud Act* (2006). According to Section 2 of the Act, an agent is in breach if he makes a false representation with the intention "to make a gain for himself or another," or "to cause loss to another or to expose another to a risk of loss."

Whistleblower Celeste Solum told Odessa Orlewicz in a March 2024 interview that she keeps a 'public-servant questionnaire' in readiness for any corporate interlopers that show up, requiring them to give their name, address, agency name, phone number, and two pieces of government-issued ID, which she then photographs. She asks them who will have access to any information she provides and on which computers the information will be stored. "These guys would come to my house and they would turn white," she told Orlewicz. "Their knees would start shaking, and they would almost wet their pants."

Also check their paperwork. According to The People's Lawyer, at thepeopleslawyeruk.com/, court bailiffs must have original court documents that include a case reference number, the court seal, and a legible wet-ink signature. We have already seen how so-called magistrates' courts in the U.K. rubber-stamp fake Liability Orders on an industrial scale for council-tax collection, meaning any paperwork coming to you likely won't meet these conditions.

Same goes for traffic fines, where fake Warrants are

churned out through centralized bulk processing without giving the extortees Due Process of Law, including the Right to a Fair Hearing. According to Vobes listener, Lizzie, corresponding with him in March 2024, you can call the Courts and Tribunal Service (HMCTS) complaint number on 0300 123 1057 to get a fake Warrant removed.

Police

If police are present, ask if they are there to see that no Breach of the Peace is committed, because a constable must arrest a bailiff for Breach of the Peace if, in the presence of the constable, he places the alleged debtor in fear of violence or harm. Also inform any police that they are required to check the identity and paperwork of your unwelcome visitors.

If the agent has claimed to be a court employee and doesn't have the certificate to verify it, or if he doesn't have a proper Warrant, the constable is required to arrest him for 'fraud by false representation' under Section 2 of the *Fraud Act*, as cited above. If it is a traffic-related claim, the *Road Traffic Act* (1991) also comes into play, where "Any person who is not a certificated bailiff but who purports to levy a distress as such a bailiff, and any person authorising him to levy it, shall be deemed to have committed a trespass" (Section 78(7)).

If a trespasser refuses to leave, the third refusal puts him in 'Aggravated Trespass', at which point you can remove him with reasonable force or order a constable to do so. If the agent is putting you in fear, they are committing Assault.

The police certainly have no business assisting bailiffs. As I pointed out in *Know Your Medical Rights*, under the *Criminal Justice and Courts Act* (2015), a British police constable who exercises his or her powers and privileges improperly is liable on conviction "to imprisonment for a term not exceeding 14 years or a fine (or both)." Under Section 26(4) of the Act, a constable's exercise of powers and privileges is improper when it is "for the purpose of achieving... a detriment for another person."

Quoting this legislation, another Richard Vobes listener named Derek points out it is illegal for police to assist anybody, including a debt-collection agent, bailiff, or enforcement officer, in debt collection. "A debt is a civil matter, and therefore not subject to police intervention. The police can only observe, and where a criminal offence has been committed and witnessed (allegations are not facts), arrest the offender. Otherwise, the police attendance is purely to keep the peace."

Derek also argues a car cannot be seized to pay a debt because the person against whom a debt is alleged is not the owner in the legal system, only the 'Registered Keeper'. The V5C registration document boldly states on the front page, "THIS DOCUMENT IS NOT PROOF OF OWNERSHIP."

THIS DOCUMENT IS NOT PROOF OF OWNERSHIP.
It shows who is responsible for registering and taxing the vehicle.

The tyrants want to have it both ways. It's not your car the rest of the time, but when it comes to paying off your alleged debts, now it *is* your 'vehicle', in effect a vehicle for revenue generation by the state. Therefore, if anyone wants to seize your car or any other asset to pay off your alleged debt, demand that they provide a Proof of Claim that you are the owner of whichever asset they want. That is difficult for them to do if documents list you only as a 'keeper' or 'tenant' , and impossible if the asset is in Trust.

As I noted in *Know Your Medical Rights,* the Constable's Oath in Britain, sworn by officers of every rank, is among the best police oaths in the world. Though it omits an important clause of forswearing membership in a secret society, it does swear to uphold "fundamental human rights" and the Law of the Land—Common Law—as it pertains to human rights.

This makes the crimes routinely committed by British police all the more egregious. They have become a legion of Oath-breakers, leading to the obvious conclusion that they are instead serving secret oaths, accompanied by conscience-killing rituals of atrocity. Therefore, they either avoid real criminals or conspire with them while devoting their empty little brains to terrorizing people who express inconvenient views on social media or who cause hurt feelings.

Forced Entry?

Forced entry into a debtor's home, whether by police or bailiffs, is utterly unlawful, of course, but it's illegal too. In Morris v Beardmore (1980), the House of Lords held that police officers have no implied authority to enter private property if the owner has explicitly forbidden them to do so, even to investigate a crime or take a breath specimen. Those that enter without permission are trespassers, and may be liable for any resulting damages or harm. The ruling quoted the finding of a lower court that "a trespassing constable ceases to be a constable in uniform."

Also be aware of the key distinction between a Warrant of Control and a Warrant of Entry, which agents are wont to conflate. As Stan, another Vobes follower explained, they are different documents that serve different purposes. A Warrant of Control authorizes an enforcement agent to take control of goods belonging to a debtor. A Warrant of Entry, on the other hand, is typically issued in relation to a criminal investigation; it authorizes a police officer to enter a property and search for evidence or to perform a particular action such as to arrest a suspect or conduct a search. Warrants of Entry are not typically used for debt-recovery cases. "So next time you get anyone claiming to have a warrant of control, be aware that this is not permission to enter your property."

Protective Court Precedents

Below, I list many more protective court precedents that I have taken from a 2016 Freedom-of-Information response from the U.K. Courts and Tribunals Development Directorate, part of HM Courts & Tribunals Service. These are echoed in a book-length article titled *The Council Tax Fraud,* published Apr. 11, 2023 by thepeopleslawyeruk.com.

- Debtors can remove implied right of access to property by telling him to leave (Davis v Lisle (1936), and McArdle v Wallace (1964)).

- A person, having been told to leave, is now under a duty to withdraw from the property with all due reasonable speed. Failing to do so, he is no longer acting in the execution of his duty and becomes a trespasser. Any subsequent levy is invalid and attracts a liability under a claim for damages (Morris v Beardmore (1980)).

- Officials cannot force their way into a private dwelling (Grove v Eastern Gas (1952)).

- An individual can use force to resist an officer from gaining entry (Weaver v Bush (1795), Simpson v Morris (1813), and Polkinhorne v Wright (1845)).

- An attempt at forcible entry despite resistance is wrongful (Ingle v Bell (1836)).

- Officers cannot apply force to a door to gain entry (Broughton v Wilkerson (1880)).

- An officer may not encourage a third party (such as workmen inside a house) to allow the officer access to a property. Access by this means renders the entry unlawful (Nash v Lucas (1867)).

- The debtor's home and all buildings within the boundary of the premises are protected against forced entry (Munroe & Munroe v Woodspring District Council (1979)).

- If a bailiff enters by force, he is there unlawfully (Curlewis v Laurie (1848), and Vaughan v McKenzie (1969)).

- If a bailiff jams his foot in the door, any levy that is subsequently made is not valid (Rai & Rai v Birmingham City Council (1993), Vaughan v McKenzie (1969), and Broughton v Wilkerson (1880)).

- A bailiff is not permitted to enter a property by improper means or by unusual routes (Ancaster v Milling (1823), and Rogers v Spence (1846)).

Having looked through these court precedents and legislation looking for crumbs of protection amid all the nasty legislated theft, I come away with a sick feeling at how rigged the game is and in imagining the trauma, torment, and stress suffered by those on the receiving end of these assaults. They demonstrate, however, the importance of heading off threats if possible before they get to the point of having thugs show up at your property.

In Closing...

I close this chapter by citing *Magna Carta* again: "We will appoint as justices, constables, sheriffs, or bailiffs only such as know the law of the realm and mean to observe it well" (Article 45). This puts to shame the legions of corrupt and unscrupulous order-followers pretending to inhabit these roles today. Ultimately, our power lies not in pleading with these psychopaths to be a little less unkind to us but in overthrowing them. If, after all the law, legal protection, and court precedent you can cite, they are still determined to be lawless, then the local community must rally to thwart them.

Remember that, as I showed in *Know Your Lawful Rights*, True Law presumes any arrest to be unlawful until the arrester proves otherwise. By the same logic, any trespass, break-in, or abduction is presumed unlawful. So, if you see a neighbour under siege by bailiffs or police, forget the uniforms, presume that the action is unlawful, and act accordingly. Neighbours, unite. Set up a low-tech alert system such as air horns to muster reinforcements. Then, if the bandits show up, you've got the numbers to repel them, arrest them, and put the intruders and Oath-breakers on trial in Common-Law courts.

8

ANY TOP-DOWN FIXES?

> *Authority lies. That is what it does... Therefore, if you, Authority, are telling me, this is what the situation is, first of all, I'm going to take it immediately that you're lying to me. My next question is, why are you lying to me? And you will know the answer to that by seeing what they say is the solution to what they're lying to you about.*
>
> — DAVID ICKE, AUGUST 2024 INTERVIEW

Throughout this series, I have focused mostly on what we can do as individuals and communities to overcome the predator class now arrayed against us. Will we go to a walled-village model, setting up Common-Law republics that later cooperate across larger regions? Or can solutions be implemented at a State level or even a national level?

In the *Solari Report on Financial Freedom* (2023), former

U.S. Assistant Secretary of Housing, Catherine Austin-Fitts, lists 17 actions individual States can take to secure financial-transaction freedom, including the formation of a State bank that would support smaller, state-based financial institutions, small businesses, and farms. It would maintain reserves in gold and silver, and there would be no taxes on precious metals nor any restrictions on using cash. The State would reject any federal funding that comes with strings attached, and it would establish telecommunications and digital communications that are protected from federal and corporate surveillance and control.

Austin-Fitts also recommends States form regional compacts with neighboring States to improve food and energy supply and resilience, while facilitating local currencies and barter networks. Her final recommendation is to train state military and militias to provide support when financial-transaction freedom is threatened, while refraining from gun-control legislation.

And what about the mythical *National Economic Security & Reformation Act* (*NESARA*), of which we hear occasional rumours? According to Nancy Detweiler, in her widely circulated *History of NESARA* article of 2011, vast gold reserves are "now safely stockpiled at the Norad Complex at Colorado Springs, Colorado and four other repositories" to be used for a new currency backed by precious metals. In 1999, Detweiler asserts, a 75-page NESARA document...

> "was submitted to Congress where it sat with little action for almost a year. Late one evening, on March 9, 2000, a written quorum call was hand-delivered by Delta Force and Navy SEALs to 15 members of the US Senate and the US House who were sponsors and co-sponsors of NESARA. They were immediately escorted by the Delta Force and Navy SEALs to their respective voting chambers where they passed the National Economic Security and Reformation Act."

Bill Clinton signed *NESARA* at gunpoint on Oct. 10, 2000, she asserts. On Sept. 11, 2001, then Fed chairman Alan Greenspan "was scheduled to announce the new US Treasury Bank system, debt forgiveness for all U.S. citizens, and abolishment of the IRS as the first part of the public announcements of NESARA," but this was thwarted by the '9/11' terrorism that unfolded that day. Since then, NESARA "remains in the background, ready to be announced."

On the face of it, the NESARA principles, as listed by Detweiler, sound like measures most of us can mostly agree on. I copy them below, then list my several objections to her narrative. NESARA...

1. Zeros out all credit card, mortgage, and other bank debt due to illegal banking and government activities. This is the Federal Reserve's worst nightmare, a "jubilee" or a forgiveness of debt.

2. Abolishes the income tax.

3. Abolishes the IRS. Employees of the IRS will be transferred into the US Treasury national sales tax area.

4. Creates a 14% flat-rate sales tax only on non-essential new items. Food and medicine will not be taxed; nor will used items such as old homes.

5. Increases benefits to senior citizens.

6. Returns Constitutional Law to all courts and legal matters.

7. Reinstates the original Title of Nobility amendment.

8. Establishes new Presidential and Congressional elections within 120 days after NESARA's announcement. The interim government will cancel all National Emergencies and return us back to Constitutional Law.

9. Monitors elections and prevents illegal election activities of special interest groups.

10. Creates a new U.S. Treasury rainbow currency [multi-coloured notes] backed by gold, silver,

and platinum precious metals, ending the bankruptcy of the United States initiated by Franklin Roosevelt in 1933.

11. Forbids the sale of American birth certificate records as chattel property bonds by the U.S. Department of Transportation.

12. Initiates new U.S. Treasury Bank System in alignment with Constitutional Law

13. Eliminates the Federal Reserve System. During the transition period the Federal Reserve will be allowed to operate side by side of the U.S. treasury for one year in order to remove all Federal Reserve notes from the money supply.

14. Restores financial Privacy.

15. Retrains all judges and attorneys in Constitutional Law.

16. Ceases all aggressive, U.S. government military actions worldwide.

17. Establishes peace throughout the world.

18. Releases enormous sums of money for humanitarian purposes.

19. Enables the release of over 6,000 patents of suppressed technologies that are being withheld from the public under the guise of national security, including free energy devices, antigravity, and sonic healing machines.

So here are my objections...

1. If this legislation was signed in 2000, and with support from some parts of the military, are we to wait another quarter of a century for its fulfilment?

2. Any top-down solution is suspect at this point. We are way past the point that the current form of Government, no matter who is in the White House or Downing Street, etc., has become destructive of Life, Liberty, and the Pursuit of Happiness, which is the trigger point for us to abolish it, according to the *Declaration of Independence*.

3. Government reform, even as broad and deep as NESARA appears to be, won't be a long-term remedy as long as Government remains in thrall to secret societies, which Detweiler doesn't even mention.

4. I find Detweiler herself to be an unreliable source, especially when she utters the

abomination that Clinton signed NESARA legislation "into law." Clueless!

5. If NESARA's implementers were truly our allies, they would not operate with the kind of secrecy and coercion that Detweiler describes, including the assassination of Senator Paul Wellstone in 2002. When so-called 'white hats' are extrajudicial assassins, where is regard for the Constitution?

6. In four places, the article calls for a return to Constitutional Law. We already have ten Lawful Amendments to the Constitution. What's lacking is not protective language but the observance and enforcement of it.

7. Principle 17 calls for "peace throughout the world." What possible objection could I have to that? Well, one-world government is a kind of peace, isn't it? But it's not the kind of peace you or I would want to live under.

As I discuss in *Know Your Medical Rights*, the devil masquerades as an angel of light, and his servants masquerade as servants of righteousness (2 *Corinthians* 11:14). Bible prophecy warns us too about...

- a king of fierce countenance who "by peace will destroy many" (*Daniel* 8:23-25);

- false prophets and wolves in sheep's clothing; fake signs and wonders to deceive "even the elect, if that were possible" (*Matthew* 24:24); and

- an alliance of two Beasts who will work together to exert totalitarian rule in a global good-cop/ bad-cop scenario (*Revelation* 13:11-18).

Bear in mind that most of the reassuring conspiracy narratives out there are designed to lull us into a false sense of security, imagining someone else will make all the bad stuff go away, so that we can be complacent again. That's not the mindset of a sovereign. I expect a change of administration in D.C. will change nothing but the paint on the door. Yes, there'll be some cosmetic window-dressing, some headline-grabbing resignations, firings, and exposures, maybe even a few anemic prosecutions, but these are the trappings of a fake saviour. After a brief honeymoon period, some new emergency will be concocted that fires up the juggernaut of tyranny assembled over the past century and more.

Ultimately, whether from a grassroots level, State level, or national level, the restoration of honest money is essential, not just for prosperity but for justice. I say "restoration," but in reality, it is hard to find any place in history where honest money was a thing. And if it was a thing, it was short-lived, for corruption in the hearts of men would always debase currencies and fractionally reserve, tax and inflate, and wage war and stage pandemics and engineer perpetual emergencies and crisis, all to siphon yet more wealth from the People.

In Closing…

I close out this chapter with the following encapsulation by British author and songwriter, Dominic Frisby, in a March 2024 conversation with James Delingpole. Having observed that the British pound lost one-third of its purchasing power during 'COVID' alone, he adds,…

> "It's nuts. While we have shit money, nothing is going to change... While a government has the power to create money at no cost to itself—which is the case in every single Western country—it is inevitable that that body will grow disproportionately large. Everyone else has to struggle to make money. Governments can just print it, they're given too much power."

True, Dominic. Through taxation and inflation, we feed the monster that feeds on us; we fund our own demise.

CONCLUSION

We're supposed to teach our children that crime doesn't pay but of course the bankers are teaching that crime does pay.

— DAVE SILVER, IN CONVERSATION WITH RICHARD VOBES, MAY 2024

I, Mr Banker, see a newborn child, and I say to myself, "Goodie, goodie. I can extract the lifeblood of this creature to make me wealthier." I label this product with an ALL-CAPS NAME, and I estimate how much can be mined from it over a lifetime.

"Mine, mine, mine," say I, the banker, so I tell Mr Government to write me a bond pledging to me its future payments, and I instruct him to proceed with taxing, fining, criminalizing, and charging this mewling, puking infant for the rest of its useless life. Then, perhaps, I decide I want to cash in early, so I sell this bond to another banker for a lump sum, and that banker takes over receipt of those payments.

Remember that, as I describe in *Know Your Lawful Rights*, the entire system of government, legislation, and banking is designed to flatten your three-dimensional existence, through a fictional STRAWMAN, into a two-dimensional realm of paper and bills and currency. That way, your three-dimensional life and labour can be extracted through two-dimensional transactions. Then, the parasite class can convert their two-dimensional takings back into three-dimensional goods and services to supply their lavish lifestyles.

Are you angry yet? This is a simplified encapsulation of the Birth-Certificate fraud. As David Icke observes, "The system is run by parasites... They don't create anything. What they do is feed off the efforts and the creativity of the population. That's what banks do. And they do it with money that doesn't exist. It's organized crime."

Now consider the game of Monopoly to see how the theft continues. If I am playing as, say, the Top Hat, and my character goes bankrupt, I the Living Man don't have to open my wallet to make good on the shortfall in the game, but in the Banker/Government game, we are required to supply our real assets, time, and wealth to top up their bottomless coffers. "They've had everything for nothing, for ever," as freedom warrior Paul Webster said in a September 2024 interview with Richard Vobes.

Webster is best known for his video presentation titled *Gas, Water & Electric Are Free to Domestic Customers*. As

I witness the long and often lonely battles he and others have fought against false authorities, knee-deep in documents, in and out of courtrooms, holding fast to Common-Law principles while poring through history, legislation, and court precedent to expose and challenge systemic fraud, I marvel at their courage, dedication, and tenacity. I feel like a bewildered novice in their presence yet knowing I must learn from them because we face an army of occupation in the form of governments, banks, and corporations, along with the secret-society networks that run them and bind them with oaths of atrocity.

I began this *Battle Manuals for Freedom series* as a rebuke to medical tyranny, but the COVID scam gave me eyes to see a bigger picture and to expose it through three books. I don't pretend to have all the answers, nor can one volume, or even three, cover all the strategies out there, much less the variations of those strategies. I am a warrior in training, and I dare say you are too, while our enemy's position has been entrenched for millennia.

But if *I* can't keep up with all the weapons designed by my freedom-loving allies, then neither will our enemies. You may well come up with your own approaches that no-one else has thought of yet. As Kayles told Richard Vobes in their November 2023 interview, "It's not written in stone. We know the deceit, we know the fraud, what's going on, so this is why there's so many different approaches people can take, and there's no right, there's no wrong."

The mockers, including so-called lawyers, will show a video of a 'sovereign-citizen' fail and try to dismiss our mission as a lie, but they are too lazy to know that the very term 'sovereign citizen' is an oxymoron. A sovereign with even a rudimentary education about his Rights, will know he is not a 'citizen'. Those scoffers also overlook the countless successes of sovereigns who have studied and trained.

Are not our legends full of tales where a famed sword chooses the warrior deemed worthy to wield it? As Si the Spaniard puts it, "You can't just pick up a template and expect that the piece of paper's going to do the job for you. That is not the behaviour of a sovereign. A sovereign takes responsibility for their actions and will thoroughly research what they're doing."

Perhaps we chose to be here on this Earth and to contend with the dark powers at such a time as this, when Bible prophecy is coming true at a pace both thrilling and alarming. This is a test, according to Si, and those who copy their homework will fail the exam.

Nor are we going to put a lawyer proxy in the exam room who will rust your weapon and blunt your edge. As I have said before, lawyers are nothing but corporate power-brokers negotiating over how much the system is going to take from you. If you have been with me through this series, you will surely agree that, as Allegedly Dave told James Delingpole, "Lawyers don't know the Law; they know the legal system. Law and the legal system are two completely different things."

In your conversations with others too, you will join me in correcting anyone who makes the blasphemous error of calling legislation 'Law'. Though I talk of

Common Law and of the Two Commandments of Christ, I will not attach to 'Law' other descriptors such as Administrative, Admiralty, Canon, Case, Commercial, Communitarian, Ecclesiastical, Equity, Fleet, Maritime, Martial, Merchant, Noahide, Papal, Roman, Sharia, Statutory, Talmudic, or Tort. Not even Constitutional, for though constitutions be generally lawful, they are still written by men.

Nor will we ask permission to stand in our Sovereignty, that is to say, to do as we see fit with our lives, loves, bodies, and possessions. That means unlearning the conditioning we have been subjected to all our lives, and seeing the Legal for what it is: Theatre. Si continues, "I try to look at all the different remedies, things that work, whether in or out of their realm."

Exactly. You can play a role *in* the Theatre of the Legal when you choose to, but you know you are not *of* the Theatre. Unlike most of Mankind, you know it is all fake, all counterfeit. You know there is an exit door from the theatre too, and do not make the mistake of thinking its scenery or special effects are real. Nor are we persuaded by comedy duos disguised as presidential debates, ghost legislation, or rumours of 'white hats', a concept no more trustworthy than the white tiles on a Freemason floor.

Again, I urge you to practise and hone discernment, both in the people you listen to and the choices you make. I have followed some social-media channels in the past, and even quoted them, who later turned out to be a 'Limited Hangout', Controlled Opposition, or at least Constrained Opposition because they self-censor out of fear or a limiting belief system. They are what David Icke calls 'the Barricade Brigade' or 'here and no further'. And then there is 'Confused Opposition', a term coined by campaigner James Roguski, which includes those who chase after distractions while missing the key issue.

This is a spiritual fight above all, and our battles in the fields of medicine, law, and banking can only be fully understood in that context. I am also on my guard against someone befriending me in order to find out what I know or to inform on me to an enemy. Varied are the devil's schemes, but we are not unaware of them.

Like me, you may feel tired of seeing evil prosper and stupidity reign, tired of trying to be heard amid a dross of indifference, and tired of watching vast swathes of stupefied Humanity marching to the cliff edge and choosing ignorance over Truth. But let us now turn our gaze together to the Author and perfecter of our faith, knowing, "We are hard pressed on every side, but not crushed; perplexed, but not in despair; persecuted, but not abandoned; struck down, but not destroyed" (2 *Corinthians* 4:8-9).

Much Love,
Abdiel LeRoy

BATTLE MANUALS FOR FREEDOM

GENI.US/RIGHTS

Book 1: *Know Your Medical Rights*

Book 2: *Know Your Lawful Rights*

Book 3: *Know Your Financial Rights*

Book 4: *Know Your Spiritual Rights*

INTRODUCTION TO 'KNOW YOUR MEDICAL RIGHTS'

BOOK 1 IN 'BATTLE MANUALS FOR FREEDOM'

I was brought up by my mother on the Bible, and she told me something that I've never forgotten. She said the stories in the Bible are stories about the conflict between the kings who have power and the prophets who preach righteousness, and she taught me to support the prophets and not the kings.

— TONY BENN, FORMER BRITISH MEMBER OF PARLIAMENT, MAR. 10, 2006

I am writing this book because I have to, and because I know a confrontation is coming. No longer can I maintain the old uneasy coexistence with false authority, lamenting his folly and fraud, deploring his ignorance, and ridiculing his absurdities, but all from a safe distance. No, I am on a collision course with false authority, and I dare say you are too. We need to be prepared.

I have lived and worked on four continents, swum in three oceans, heard innumerable foreign tongues, and observed the infinite variety of our species, but now the autocrats, bureaucrats, and technocrats, in their little, brief, and fear-fueled authority, would have us undergo invasive medical procedures, and hand over private medical information once held sacred, just to travel, to go about our lives, and even to make a living.

Time was when I could grudgingly accept mask requirements in the early days, frown at destructive lockdowns, and ignore voicemails and messages to my mobile phone from Britain's National Health Service (NHS). And I could largely dismiss the barrage of fearmongering propaganda that managed to circumvent my longstanding aversion to mainstream media. But when governments started threatening and penalizing bodily autonomy, a line was crossed.

I know in my heart that these measures are an atrocity, and my spirit rebels against them, but just having that instinct is not enough now. **WHAT ARE MY RIGHTS?!** I'm going to need more than mere disgust if I am to overrule the fearmongering autocrats who will exploit any emergency to unleash tyranny. I'm going to need constitutional armour and weapons of law, and I'm going to need them quickly. And when I have them, I will share them with those who may benefit.

Hence this book, a garment of protection for the 'COVID' era and an antidote to fear. I don't mean fear of a disease, but of the reactions—or rather overreactions—to it. Though I once entertained some background anxiety about a supposed virus, it's as nothing compared to the deep dread I've experienced about a totalitarian state emerging such as Orwell set out in *1984*.

I have also come to realize that even *that* kind of fear is being stoked by governments. At the outset, they wanted us to fear COVID, but after that got them only so far, now they want us to fear them, so that we won't make trouble.

For that type of fear, I recall the predicament of Moses' Israelites lately released from slavery in Egypt, as recounted in the Bible book of *Exodus*. Imagine their terror to realize Pharaoh's entire army was bearing down on them as they approached the Red Sea (14:10). But Moses told them not to fear, to stand firm, for they would see the Lord's deliverance. And they did, when the Red Sea drowned Pharaoh and his horde (14:28).

Therefore, no matter how bad things appear to get, the final chapter of our story sees the demise of slavery on Earth, including wage slavery, debt slavery, tax slavery, prison slavery, sex slavery, digital slavery and, of course, medical slavery, along with the deaths of tyrant politicians, bureaucrats, and corporate profiteers when, like a mighty river, Justice returns.

The 'vaccines', too, have an obvious allegory in the *Exodus* story. When Moses and his brother Aaron come to Pharaoh's court and issue their demands, Aaron demonstrates the power of God by turning his staff into a snake. Pharaoh's conjurors imitate the act, but Aaron's snake eats their snakes (7:12). Similarly, the fanged creatures of Pfizer, Moderna, AstraZeneca, and Johnson & Johnson are no match for the lethal bite of truth-tellers, prophets, and whistleblowers today.

Also destined for destruction are the media organizations who have mouthpieced for the medical-industrial complex. I shudder to recall the *Daily Telegraph* front-page headline of July 21, 2021: "Freedom for double jabbed as UK opens to world." As if freedom can be granted or withheld at official whim, as if medical status were the qualification to receive it. No, we are born with it, and trying to take it away from us is blasphemy, no less an atrocity than the 'intercision' of Philip Pullman's novel, *The Golden Compass*, where the authorities cut children away from their 'daemon' animals, equivalent to extracting their souls.

The *Telegraph* also predicted, in a July-2021 article, "The unvaccinated will be shut out of normal life, progressively demonised, and stripped of civil rights..." And other mainstream outlets salivated at the prospect. As 2021 drew to a close, a quick glance at recent headlines showed an almost desperate eagerness to foment hatred against a vilified underclass. "The unvaccinated are putting us all at risk," squealed *The Times* of London. "I'm Furious at the Unvaccinated," howled *The New York Times*. "It is only a matter of time before we turn on the unvaccinated," thundered *The Guardian*.

Just like the cultist politicians and bureaucrats, these media mercenaries for Big Pharma know not what they say or what they do. Nor do they know or care that international statute defines persecution against an identifiable group as a Crime Against Humanity. Have all these puppets learned nothing from history and the madness of going after a targeted minority? Has it taken but a few generations to overturn what our ancestors fought and died for? Have these people lost their minds? I think they have!

We of prophetic calling have our work cut out for us, not just seeing, or warning against, future scenarios, as exemplified by Orwell, but in describing the present. That means observing the obvious and stating the obvious when populations are conditioned to overlook the obvious, to deny it to themselves and, even if they do see it, to keep quiet about it. As famed whistleblower Edward Snowden observes, "Everywhere we look, from Afghanistan to economics, from pandemic to pervasive surveillance, the obvious has been made unspeakable."[i]

And it is obvious that the medical-industrial complex, taking its playbook from the *military*-industrial complex, grooms politicians to do its bidding. It also likens the COVID response to war, reflecting the imperial and imperious mindset infecting our politics, with words like battle, beat, conquer, crush, defeat, eliminate, enemy, fight, front lines, victory, etc.

There *is* a war being waged, certainly, but of a very different kind, as encapsulated by the apostle Paul in the New Testament: "For our struggle is not against flesh and blood, but against the rulers, against the authorities, against the powers of this dark world and against the spiritual forces of evil in the heavenly realms" (*Ephesians* 6:12).

And those spiritual forces are especially murderous towards children, recalling the ancient abomination of child sacrifice to Molech.

> "The Lord said to Moses, 'Say to the Israelites: Any Israelite or any foreigner residing in Israel who sacrifices any of his children to Molek is to be put to death. The members of the community are to stone him. I myself will set my face against him and will cut him off from his people; for by sacrificing his children to Molek, he has defiled my sanctuary and profaned my holy name. If the members of the community close their eyes when that man sacrifices one of his children to Molek and if they fail to put him to death, I myself will set my face against him and his family and will cut them off from their people, together with all who follow him in prostituting themselves to Molek.' "
>
> — *LEVITICUS* 20:1-5

Of course, fraud, corruption, and greed have always greased the wheels of government, but now we observe something far deadlier, a medical cult that demands human sacrifice, a religion of death, served by a conclave of tyrant priests in positions of false authority. The more they can kill, the higher they rise in their infernal ranks.

I wish the figureheads of our so-called 'medical-freedom movement' would see this. I wish they would realize that the pharmaceutical complex is not so much counting the dollars as it is counting the bodies.

I came to this realization when hearing renowned liver-health specialist and author, Dr. Burt Berkson, tell Dr. Jonathan Landsman in an interview, "At many medical schools, in many university hospitals, they give an award every month to the doctor who has the most deaths on his service, and they have a party, and it's called a 'Black Crow Award'."

Is that what this is all about? Are we in the middle of a global Black Crow Award now, in which medical professionals and hospitals and so-called health ministers are competing to see who can add the most corpses to the pile of medical waste? Or have they been assigned kill quotas?

That medical-freedom leaders overlook this deeper motivation is disappointing, but many more errors, and possibly fatal ones, they make besides. Most dangerous of all is to base their opposition to medical compulsion not on the solid ground that it is eternally unlawful, but on the shifting sands of data and statistics.

For example, they argue that this disease, or that variant, is too mild to warrant medical enforcements. Meaning what? That if some more deadly disease were conjured, they'd be fine with coercion?

That is boggy ground to build on, to paraphrase Herman Melville. Of course, autocrats are always ready to unleash another emergency which they will cite as pretext for more crackdowns and despotic legislation that they falsely call 'law'.

We also hear the medical-freedom caucus arguing certain measures should not be mandated because they are unproven, unsafe, or ineffective. Or because natural immunity is a thing, or asymptomatic spread is not a thing.

Fools! There is no 'because'! No medical measure can ever be compulsory—period, end of—whatever claims are asserted for its safety or effectiveness.

And here's the stupidest slogan of all. "Where there is risk, there must be choice." Meaning what? That if some medical treatment is concocted, and safety claimed for it, then choice can be taken away?

Misguided, too, are requests for 'exemption' from medical enforcement. These buy into a fiction that government has authority to demand anything from us in the first place. It doesn't. Quite the opposite. We have authority over government, and the word "No" is, always has been, and always will be, exemption enough.

Exemption requests also desecrate medical confidentiality when your medical status is nobody else's business in the first place. It is not the government's business, not your employer's business, not a travel company's business, and not your neighbour's business. Respect confidentiality, and your medical status can never be weaponized against you.

Our resolve against medical dictatorship, therefore, can never rest on competing views about today's data and circumstances but must instead be anchored in **CONSTITUTIONALITY**. Blind to emergency by design, constitutional principles are eternal and can't be swayed by the shifting currents of perception and statistics. They don't give a fuck about conditions on the ground, and nor should they. No, these times call us to be **CONSTITUTIONAL EXTREMISTS**.

Lawyers, too, need to grasp this. They whimper about not being able to go after pharmaceutical companies, doctors, hospitals, or regulators because of 'legal immunity'. Servile creatures, I rebuke your compliance with tyrant fictions spun to enslave Mankind. The Acts and statutes you cite—and stop calling them laws—these licences to kill, are nothing more than corporate contracts that one party has drafted, one party has signed, and one party has negotiated with itself. Yet that party thinks to impose those contracts on another party, us, to codify enslavement, murder, extortion, destruction, and theft, and then to pardon itself of the crimes. As we shall see, in the coming section on Common Law, these instruments are powerless without our signature, and not worth the air they're written on.

Imagine you were a business owner seeking to procure goods from a supplier, but that supplier gets to write the contract without your review, and that contract binds you as soon as the ink is dry without your knowledge, signature, or consent. You'd tell them to get lost, wouldn't you? Yet that is precisely the bargain that governments and their corporate conspirators think to impose, and before which our conditioned cadre of cringing lawyers think to kneel. When will you stop enthroning legislation over Justice?!

One rare exception to this tendency is British human-rights lawyer, Anna de Buisseret. Interviewed in London's Parliament Square during a Medical Freedom March of Oct. 30, 2021, she advises:

> "Learn what your fundamental, inalienable human rights are. Anyone who can access Google, you google the Universal Declaration of Human Rights, read it, read the European Convention on Human Rights, read the U.K. Human Rights Act, read the International Covenant on Social and Political and Economic Rights. Those rights are all there. It's all there in the law. The reason this is happening is because people don't know the law, so they don't know how to uphold it and assert it."

I applaud the spirit of her words, though that's an awful lot of homework for your average freedom-loving reader to do, especially if you add in the 170-page Notice of Liability, prepared by de Buisseret and her allies in Lawyers for Liberty, to serve against skin piercers and their accomplices. But I *have* done the homework and distilled into this book the key language that empowers us.

The good news is that none of this is complicated. It doesn't require a law degree, nor a thorough grounding in Latin. The beauty of these universal principles lies in their plain-English simplicity and, like the proverbial mustard seed of faith that overthrows mountains,[ii] our little understanding in this arena goes a long way in vaulting the pronouncements of foolish and fearful men.

A layman's expertise will do, and a layman's analysis can provide it, which is why I am as qualified as anyone else to do so here.

Brothers and sisters, it is time to release from their glass cabinets the dusty scrolls of our Rights declarations. We reclaim the keys that unleash them and, like the true prophets of old, proclaim them again to break the spells and incantations of false priests now roaming the Earth.

Our Rights, being inalienable, or unalienable if you prefer, were never granted by a gift of government nor rescinded by a denial of government. In the words of John K. Webster, creator of the documentary *Strawman,*

> **"GOVERNMENT IS A CREATION OF MAN, AND A CREATION OF MAN CAN NEVER BE ABOVE MAN."**

So, if governments will not hear or heed the simple and time-honoured constitutional principles they are sworn to uphold, then each of us must acquire at least a little expertise in this area.

Nor will I pin my hopes on a political party or candidate to produce a regime a little less vindictive than the last. Love for our Rights straddles the old divides where antagonists are merely co-conspirators in bipartisan acts of theft. As Martin Luther wrote of the papists and anabaptists in 1531, "These foxes are tied together by the tails, even though their heads look in opposite directions. While they outwardly profess to be great enemies, inwardly they think, teach, and defend one and the same thing." Once we realize this, and expose the unholy alliances against our core values, whether by Democrat with Republican, Tory with Labour, or by any other duopoly or coalition, we can be rid of this corrupt political theatre altogether.

We are in a Declaration-of-Independence moment when an entire *form* of government, not just a faction *within* government, is destroying Life, Liberty, and the Pursuit of Happiness. It is therefore our duty now to abolish *this* form of government, maybe even the entire *idea* of government (which means 'mind control'). We are not fighting in a horizontal plane of 'Left' versus 'Right', but in the vertical plane of Life over Death, Creation over Destruction, Love over Fear.

That is a spiritual battle, the battle for which this book is conceived. May this declaration in words empower us to "suit the action to the word, the word to the action"[iii] as we hear and heed the rallying call from the Captain of our souls, he whose Word "is alive and active, and sharper than any double-edged sword" (*Hebrews* 4:12).

Similarly, the sword of constitutional truth now pulses with Heaven's call for Justice, imparting courage to those who wield it, and thirsts for the blood of today's cabal of thieves and murderers, whether in government, media, or any other organization. Let us pursue them with the kind of fury that Elijah wielded in slaughtering the false prophets of Baal on Mount Carmel (*1 Kings* 18:40). For, as Dave Mason writes in his masterful *Age of Prophecy* novels,[iv] set in the time of Elijah, "Those who show mercy to the cruel, bring cruelty upon the merciful."

For those of us contemplating our first run-in with would-be enforcers such as police, the task ahead may appear daunting, but here I share the vital information we will need if menaced by state or corporation, and if you have a paperback version, I hope it shall become marked up with your highlights and scribblings. Our quest may seem to present impossible odds. Well, you would have said the same of Moses and Aaron going up against Pharaoh, his court, his paymasters, slave masters, chariots, and weaponry. But he who was in the prophets was greater than he who was in Pharaoh, and he who is in us now is greater than he who is in the autocrats, bureaucrats, technocrats, and 'psychocrats' of our age. And, oh yes, the 'philanthrocrats' too!

"Hold the line, stand your ground, uphold the rule of law, step into your sovereignty," De Buisseret urges in the closing moments of her Parliament-Square interview. "The law is all there to protect you, but you're not going to get protected unless you know what it is and you uphold it."

Therefore, we look to the eternal values of Mankind—values not swayed by political convenience and expediency, nor by profiteering motives, and that have *more* currency, not less, during times of emergency, whether that emergency is real or perceived or invented. So join me in the field, my friend. These times will make prophets of us all!

---

i. Addressing the Belmarsh Tribunal that examined state crimes against Julian Assange, Oct. 22, 2021.
ii. *Matthew* 17:20.
iii. Shakespeare, *Hamlet*, III.ii.
iv. At the time of going to press, the first novel in this series, titled *The Lamp of Darkness*, was free in eBook version at various on-line retailers.

INTRODUCTION TO 'KNOW YOUR LAWFUL RIGHTS'

BOOK 2 IN 'BATTLE MANUALS FOR FREEDOM'

The elite's goal is disturbingly straightforward: to hollow out the individual, leaving an empty shell while stripping away the soul.

— A LILY BIT, *THE EXPOSE*, MAR. 15, 2024

We were born into slavery, but until recently, most of us did not know it. With subtle treachery, banks, corporations, and governments have stolen our Birthright. Spiritual vampires, they have drained us of our time and energies, even of life itself, to enrich themselves. It took the atrocities of COVID to alert us to this, to shake us awake, and to break the spell that has been perpetrated against Mankind for centuries and even millennia.

Some were aware of the tyrants' genocidal plans even

before COVID, and for that you have my deepest respect. You did your best to warn everyone what evil was afoot, and you saved lives. Though you were censored and reviled, you stuck to your message, and then I joined you to expose how broad and deep is the conspiracy against us. In early 2022, I published *The COVID Protocols: Upholding Your Rights in Authoritarian Times,* now retitled *Know Your Medical Rights.* I thought this would be enough, but when the despotism spread from the medical arena to every other area of life, I realized COVID was just the first round in a barrage of assaults aimed at demolishing our lives, our livelihoods, and all that makes life worth living. I would need to write more books.

I agree with Dr. Rima Laibow's observation, in a March 2024 interview with Maria Zeee, that...

> "There is no aspect of human life which will be allowed to continue as we know it, as we value it. And most of all, what is being destroyed is the capacity to love and to trust one another. So we are being separated from our wisdom, from our bodies, from our DNA, from our children, from our property, from our very capacity to bring food forth from the Earth. We are being separated from our ability to think, to communicate, all of it in the interest of a vast and total suppression of humanity into a slave caste that can never rise up again. To which my response is, 'No! Out! I want out of your system!' "

Yes, Dr. Rima has poetically described the breadth of tyranny now afoot, but I am astonished too by its depth.

It starts with international puppet masters, usually described as 'globalists', who take their orders from secret societies and the infernal influences that inspire them. Then, the tyranny is channeled through their network of despots installed in national governments and other corporations.

The infestation doesn't stop there, though, for regional and local governments, county councils, town councils, planning departments, and even school boards and housing associations are fully on board with the despotic agenda of enslavement and destruction, either as complicit operatives or as useful idiots.

Police forces, meanwhile, corporate henchmen and bandits for hire, are enforcing all of this. How refreshing it would be if just one stood up and said, "No sir. That's an unlawful order." What a revelation if just one upheld their Oath. Instead, we are treated to the shameful spectacle of police beating up, trampling, and irradiating protesters, menacing journalists, arresting people for praying in public, and even issuing tickets against those who feed the homeless. And that's just what they do in public. Meanwhile, they give protective escort to today's agents of doom when angry crowds come too close.

COVID also taught me a new word: democide, defined in the *Collins Dictionary* as "the killing of members of a country's civilian population as a result of its government's policy, including by direct action, indifference, and neglect." I now realize that governments of the West have been doing this for decades, but they got much more unsubtle and extreme about it with COVID, both with the murderous protocols deployed in hospitals and nursing homes, then with the coerced poison injections they called 'vaccines'. Since then, among many vectors of attack, they have gone after our food, our fuel, and funds too.

I laugh when I hear people talk about "government overreach" or when they say, "The government doesn't have your best interests at heart." OK, I suppose you could call genocide 'overreach', but strip away the varnish and you will see a regime that wants to enslave you, to extract every ounce of value it can from your life and labour then, when you've nothing left to give, to discard you as cheaply as possible and add your corpse to the growing pile of medical waste. And if that's too much of a mouthful, your government simply wants to kill you!

Nor are legislators doing much to check rogue administrations. As 'Health Ranger' Mike Adams said in a May 2024 broadcast,...

> "All they do every single day in the halls of Congress is they figure out, 'How can we hurt America today? How do we harm the American people? How do we vote against the interests of the American people?' They're straight-up traitors. Every single day, they conspire of how to destroy this country from within."

And that conspiracy is entirely 'legal' in the sense that politicians, or rather their handlers, have drawn up documents that not only codify their thefts and murders but shield them from consequence with so-called 'legal immunity'. I tend to agree with Max Igan's encapsulation, in a February 2024 broadcast, that "Every single problem on Earth exists because it has been legislated to exist."

Which brings me to a central theme of this book, and that is to draw a clear distinction between 'legal' and 'lawful', for they are very different things and usually contrary. 'Legal' pertains to the legislation that men create—Acts, statutes, rules, regulations, decrees, and codes, the injustice of which corporate courts cement with their rulings. 'Lawful', by contrast, belongs only to the Creator, whom to serve is Freedom (*John* 8:36; 2 *Corinthians* 3:17) and whose burden is light (*Matthew* 11:28-30), and it respects our inherent Rights and dignity. These Rights may be enshrined in constitutions but they don't depend on constitutions for their existence or applicability.

As Living Men and Women operating in the Lawful, which is our Birthright, we are wholly above the Legal. Indeed, as three-dimensional beings, we are an entire *dimension* above the Legal, which operates only in the two-dimensional realm of words on paper. Those words cannot reach up from the page, grab us by the neck, and pull us down into their flattened space, though that is what their devisers intend. No, those documents are dead to us, and we refuse to breathe life into them by consenting to them with our signatures. In the three-dimensional realm where we live and move and breathe and have our beings, Government cannot even touch us, much less dictate to us.

Yet politicians, along with enforcers and

commentators, routinely ascribe to tyrant code the false label of 'Law'. It's all fiction, all counterfeit. By True Law, or 'Common Law', those who deliberately do harm must face Justice, while the falsely accused are innocent if there is no victim.

More troubling still, the fallacy of calling rules made up by men and women 'Law' is echoed by so-called alternative voices, Freedom warriors, and 'truthers' who should know better. This one error has me "shouting at the radio" more than any other.

For example, Katherine Watt, whose work I respect, routinely makes the mistake of calling legislation 'Law', so does Sasha Latypova. I have heard James Delingpole, Catherine Austin Fitts, Peggy Hall, Greg Reese, James Roguski, Jane Ruby, Scott Schara, and Maria Zeee all err on this point. Mike Adams makes this error in almost every episode of his Health Ranger Report, and Todd Callender in almost every sentence.

I respect their research, but through this one abuse of language alone, they unwittingly confer on governments a false authority to play God in the lives of others; dictate to us what we must do with our bodies, our property, our children, and even out thoughts; and then have us bend the knee and plead for 'exemptions' that they may grant at their pleasure by a counterfeit mercy.

Lawyers, too, are generally taking government writ as gospel by confining their range of motion to the shrinking legal box of legislation. Even to call them 'lawyers' is a misnomer when, for the most part, they are not dealing in Law at all but in the muck of legislation. They are not lawyers but corporate power-brokers and negotiators cutting deals with corporate entities, wherein you and I are regarded as no more than corporations.

So, if there's only one thing you take away from this book, let it be this...

STOP CALLING LEGISLATION LAW!

This one shift in mindset will produce good fruit. You will see legislation for the toilet fodder it really is, and even 'legislation' may be too generous a term because the entities that forge it, pretend to debate it, and dutifully pass it are all corporations, that is to say, invented things, and their prolixious documents amount to nothing more than corporate policy, binding only upon themselves and their own employees. All governments, parliaments, courts, and police forces *are* corporations, and their policies, procedures, and decrees have no more authority over us than if McDonald's or Starbucks had written them.

It boils down to this: God makes Law, man makes legislation, and corporations make company policy. How dare they ascribe to men and to the institutions of men the authority to make Law? When there is already so little airtime afforded genuine voices for Freedom, we cannot afford to build on such a broken foundation.

Further, Acts and statutes are, in effect, contracts that one party draws up, one party negotiates with itself, and one party signs, and then thinks to impose on another party, us, without our signature or consent, much less our

Informed Consent. Governments and corporations may not impose any demand on you unless you have voluntarily, and with full knowledge, signed a contract that includes your agreement to the demand. Therefore, if some would-be enforcer tells you, "You have to do this. This is the law," you say, "Show me the document that says this, and show me where I signed it."

Still, I wrestled with calling this book, *Know Your Legal Rights* instead of *Know Your Lawful Rights.* Though the Lawful is as far above the Legal as the heavens are above the Earth, we may on occasion operate in the Legal, and though we are not subject to the pieces of paper written by men, we may still cite them on a Legal stage to compel enforcers to obey the contracts binding upon themselves.

If we enter the Legal, therefore, we do so as an actor puts on a costume to play a role. We do not *live* in the Legal, any more than an actor would live his entire life in the costume and lines of his character, but we may play a role in it sometimes. Imagine the hell of an actor trapped forever in the fictional time and place of his theatrical persona with no way out, even worse if he lost all memory of his prior life outside the role and forgot there was an exit. That nightmarish condition describes much of Humanity today, but not you or me. If we ever operate in the Legal, we remember that we are not *of* the Legal.

In the end, I went with *Lawful* for the title, because that is the realm of Truth, whereas Legal is the realm of fiction. Like a thieving usurper, Legal has crept into the throne room of our Sovereignty and presumes to rule as

King, but he is an impostor and must be ousted if we are to restore our Birthright in the Lawful.

This requires a shift in mindset. We have much to learn, or rather unlearn, as we dismantle the lies, programming, and conditioning that have kept us from ourselves. The walls of my own perception too must dissolve to write this book. Ironically, COVID did much of that work for me by exposing the evil, and the doers of that evil, that have long crouched in the shadows and quietly infested our institutions. As the poet Theodore Roethke wrote, "In a dark time the eye begins to see." I imagine God's hand on the dimmer switch of our awareness and gradually turning up the light.

And as that dawn returns, Government shall no longer be enthroned in the minds of men, nor shall its ideologies, stupidity, or stupid ideologies. Alas, the evildoers have been assisted in their acts of theft and destruction by a largely compliant population. People seem to have embedded in their consciousness, "I must obey Government," turning it into a religion. Even after the COVID era, with its ample demonstration that Government is a cult seeking our enslavement and death, this idea is still firmly lodged in most people.

For example, I notice when taking flights in the U.S. that I am the only one refusing the body-scan chambers that the Transport and Security Administration (TSA) puts people through, the photos taken after international arrivals, and the biometric scans even at departure gates, all of which are Fourth-Amendment violations and, in the case of the body scans, medical violations too. Seeing the compliance of others is deeply frightening to me because they will passively watch tyranny happen to others and just stand idly by, or perhaps get out their mobile phones to record it and win coveted clicks on social media. At their worst, they will turn in their neighbours, or even other family members, and report non-compliance to the authorities.

I also recently saw a New Zealand honey producer torching his hives and with them, millions of bees, because the government told him to. Before that, an Australian producer allowed government agents on to his property where they drowned his bees in petrol. It is an enraging spectacle. The bees, at least, have enough regard for their own survival to sting their attackers, but many compliant humans have no sting of their own, even when directly assailed.

In Britain, meanwhile, households keeping even a single chicken are "required" to register their bird. To anyone paying even perfunctory attention, it is obvious the government will at some point try to use this information to destroy every last vestige of independent food production by conjuring some disease scare such as 'bird flu' and culling yet more hens.

Why do people keep falling for these deceptions? I want to shake them and say, "Moron, the government is trying to destroy you and your business, and the food supply along with it!" And if the autocrats can't entirely cause starvation, they are doing their best to destroy independent farmers who might produce clean, healthy food. That way, they can force consumption of their highly processed, poison-laced megacorporation stomach fillers sold in supermarkets which, in turn, are extremely vulnerable to supply-line sabotage.

Even the very word, 'Government'—which means 'mind control'—is offensive to me now. Who do these people think they are to 'govern' anyone, let alone to tax us, especially when they operate in, and are promoted by, a system that rewards corruption, laziness, and incompetence, in a culture of failing upwards? As Christ said of the Pharisees in his day, "they bind heavy burdens and grievous to be borne, and lay them on men's shoulders, but do not lift a finger to help them" (*Matthew* 23:4).

In Jesus' day, the Pharisees were a hypocritical religious cult, whitewashed tombs full of dead men's bones as he described them, a brood of vipers who strain out gnats but swallow camels (*Matthew* 23). Similarly, today's Pharisees strain out gnats by punishing speech that offends them while swallowing camels of rape, genocide, and theft. Meanwhile, their religion demands of us extortionate tithes, offerings, sacrifices, and ritual performances as, almost every day, they issue some new decree to control us, some new fine or some new fee, and then expect us dutifully to follow and to obey, to follow and to pay.

In the process, our constitutions and Rights declarations are routinely trampled in the name of virtue-signalling slogans such as 'diversity', 'equity', 'inclusion', 'prevention', 'safety', 'security', 'sustainability', and so on. These are empty words when they come from the mouths of tyrants and, as Homer reminds us in *The Odyssey*, "Empty words are evil" (XI.544).

We must therefore reclaim our inherent authority and remember the obvious and irrefutable truth, as stated in the documentary *Strawman*, that "Government is a creation of Man, and a creation of Man can never be above Man." You and I have authority over every thing that Government is and every thing that Government creates. That's just the authority of logic, but Christians have the even more potent authority from our Lord and Saviour to "overcome all the power of the enemy" (*Luke* 10:19), and in case you haven't realized it, governments *are* the enemy.

So I try never to forget, should I face official, police officer, or judge, that I have authority over them and that I am the one giving *them* 'lawful orders', not the other way round, and that, like their father the devil, these operatives must flee when resisted (*James* 4:7). With this book, I am giving shape to that resistance, assembling not just our constitutional weapons but, for those who "put on the full armour of God" (*Ephesians* 6:13), our spiritual weapons too.

I will admit the enormity of this task feels daunting sometimes, for the subject is vaster than any one author can encompass. I do not pretend to have all the answers, and some of my analysis may yet be naive. Just untangling the history of how we got here would take several volumes, delving back even to Biblical times, but what I can do is present the conceptual frameworks to reclaim our Rights, dispel the illusions that have tried to imprison us, fortify your heart for the battles and skirmishes ahead, and introduce you to solutions and solvers.

I also want to minimize the cost and dangers of the non-compliance we must embrace if we want to get through this. Your instincts are already telling you not to comply, and you may be willing to sacrifice for the cause, but let us be smart about our non-compliance, disciplined, and prepared. Let us also be open to learning more, and honing our skills, as time passes, for these are early days in clawing back our Sovereignty.

The God Stuff

Now, having got Biblical with you a few times by now, I recall that some readers objected to my Scriptural references in *Know Your Medical Rights.* If that is you, season your skepticism a while and acknowledge that even our enemies are deeply religious and that their destructive influence cannot be otherwise explained. For example, do they lie? Then entertain the possibility that they serve the Father of Lies (*John* 8:44). Do they couch their tyranny in virtue-signalling language? Then ask if they serve he who masquerades as an angel of light (*2 Corinthians* 11:14-15). Do they persecute those who tell the truth and who try to warn others? Then consider if they worship he who accuses the righteous (*Revelation* 12:10). And, are they predatory? Then witness how they take after the devil who "prowls around like a roaring lion looking for someone to devour" (*1 Peter* 5:8).

Ask yourself, too, if the assaults against our bodies—not just from venomous injections but from poisons in our food, water, air, sea, and land—are motivated by a hatred of the Most High in whose image we are made (*Genesis* 1:26-27).

Also, do they act in concert across nations, writing the same legislation, telling the same lies, and issuing the same decrees, all at the same time? Then consider how they must be coordinating in secret, making secret oaths and secret pacts, and that secret oaths are the currency of secret societies such as Freemasonry. Have you observed officials, elected or otherwise, along with doctors, judges, and police, desecrating their public oaths, whether to the Constitution or Oath of Office, Hippocratic Oath, or Constable's Oath? Could that mean they are instead cleaving to secret oaths? Would you describe them as psychopaths, meaning they can kill, loot, steal, and destroy others, including children, without remorse? Then is it possible their consciences have been seared (*1 Timothy* 4:1-2) during initiation rites of atrocity? You and I have empathy enough to imagine ourselves in someone else's shoes if they tell us we are causing them harm, but that mechanism has been annihilated in the politicians and bureaucrats of today.

And if you are disposed to excuse the naive ranks of secret-society orders, where the higher-ups—or rather, the lower-downs of an inverted pyramid—conceal the real agenda from initiates, know that even at the First Degree of Freemasonry, they have already condemned themselves by an oath of atrocity. As reported at evangelicaltruth.com, the initiate swears to secrecy "under no less a penalty than that of having my throat cut across, my tongue torn out by its roots, and buried in the rough sands of the sea at low-water mark."

Therefore, show me a Freemason who purports to be a Christian, and I will show you a child of Hell. Christ warned us that no-one can serve two masters, for he will love one and despise the other (*Matthew* 6:24). We infer that the Hell-spawn of today are not just ignoring their public oaths but actively hating them, and that they hate the *Bill of Rights, Magna Carta,* and every other righteous text. Christ also warned that these traitors would plead their good works to him at the Judgment, to which he will reply, "Away from me. I never knew thee!" (*Matthew* 7:22-23).

Meanwhile, you may observe how governments are serving dogmas that try to turn reality upside-down, even going beyond Orwell's "War is peace. Freedom is slavery. Ignorance is strength." In their worldview, good is evil and evil good, love is hate and hate love, health is sickness and sickness health, male is female and female male, truth is lies and lies are truth. Democracy is dictatorship, food is starvation, medicine poison, and justice injustice. Child protection is child trafficking, and to serve and protect is to extort and destroy.

Also, when it comes to climate-change deceptions, hot is cold and cold is hot. If you find this last element jolting, note how the climate-change narrative has followed the same playbook as COVID: take a threat that is negligible or non-existent and inflate it into a harbinger of planetary doom. To bring about such overthrows of reason requires a constant barrage of indoctrination, censorship, propaganda, fear-mongering, and psychological torture, areas where so-called 'intelligence agencies' have long honed their dark arts.

With such intense attack in the arena of ideas, and with ideas being broadcast through the invisible medium of the air, might you infer this is a spiritual battle too? Do you sense a malevolent spiritual entity or network behind the scenes? Might you call that entity Satan or Lucifer? And if such an impostor set up a throne and called himself God or Messiah, would that not be the king of all inversions?

Still, I venture that you and I are so *over* state-sanctioned lies by now that the tyrants have given up trying to persuade us. Yet they must still convince *themselves*, if only to quell any protest from Conscience. "Uncertain way of gain," to quote Shakespeare's *Richard III*, "but I am in/ So far in blood that sin will pluck on sin./ Tear-falling pity dwells not in this eye" (IV.ii).

Meanwhile, if you harbour distrust of Christians, bear in mind that not all who *call* themselves Christians are truly members of the Body of Christ. Some are wolves in sheep's clothing or, calling on Shakespeare again, beautiful tyrants, fiends angelical, dove-feathered ravens, honorable villains, serpent hearts (*Romeo and Juliet*, III.ii). And some are false prophets, eager to share what "God told me."

Beware, too, of 'Controlled Opposition', those tasked with drawing dissidents into a 'Limited Hangout' that refuses to look at deeper and more horrid realities. Keep your wits about you, practise discernment, and sniff out the spiritual rot of these whitewashed tombs full of dead men's bones (*Matthew* 23:27).

But seek out those who genuinely *are* in Christ and who have chosen his ultimate authority over the false authority of men. We Christians may be all that is standing between you and annihilation. Have you noticed how Christian voices have taken the lead in recent years in denouncing and exposing the perpetrators? When, since the days of Moses or Joshua, has there been such a need for a fierce Christian army?

Do not resent your protectors, who are already paying a price for our faith. As Harrison Smith observed in a May 2024 interview with Maria Zeee, Christianity is under attack today because it impedes the totalitarian agenda...

> "It makes it hard to control people. It makes it hard to deceive and manipulate. When the whole society is sincerely righteous and desires truth and desires justice, then you can't get away with things very easily. You have to have a whole system that's corrupt and fallen, and then it makes it easy to scam, it makes it easy to get one over. They want the dog-eat-dog world where they can screw somebody over and destroy them and suffer no consequences. So Christianity is a barrier to control, it's a barrier to oppression. **It gives you something higher than earthly authority, and that naturally pisses off the earthly authority**" (emphasis mine).

Speaking of earthly authority, I will not pin my hopes on a political solution to our woes. The *Declaration of Independence* doesn't tell us to "abolish" this or that political party or political candidate, nor does it call on us to favour one traitor, despot, pussy-grabber, or paedophile over another. No, it is our "duty" to abolish any *form* of Government that is destructive of Life, Liberty, and the Pursuit of Happiness.

Many more people are aware now that political parties oppose each other in only the most superficial ways, but when it comes to matters that really affect our lives, they are firm allies in trying to despoil us. As Mike Adams observed, in an April 2024 article,...

> "The Democrats have actively destroyed this once-great nation, but the Republicans were either wholly complicit or stood by and did nothing while the arsonists set fire to the pillars of our constitutional republic. As is now obvious to anyone paying attention, we no longer have a functioning civil society in the United States of America. We have a failed government, failed election integrity, a failed justice system, a failed counterfeit currency, fake corporate media, fake war propaganda, a failed educational system, and a weaponized system of science and medicine that literally develops and deploys biological weapons against the American people."

Why do politicians act in concert against us, no matter what party they're in? Because, deep down, they're not really Democrats or Republicans, Conservatives or Labour, or whatever. These are just convenient labels for their sham political theatre. No, they serve but one party, and that is the party of Freemasonry. According to Bible scholar David Carrico, in a November 2019 episode of *Now You See TV*,...

> "If you look at the Democratic Party and the Republican Party, if you look close enough, both are Masonically controlled... These two American political parties, they are just the expression of two Masonic philosophies that both have the same ultimate goal, and that will be the New World Order."

That's why petitions and protests are useless when you're dealing with them. So too are polls when they have no compunction about rigging elections. As Max Igan observes, "There's nobody you can vote in. There's nobody you can vote out. There's no political remedy to this system."

True, Max. There is no political remedy, but other remedies are at hand. That's why I have written this book, a battle manual for warriors determined to overthrow tyrants of every stripe. One way or another, we must reclaim our Sovereignty, our freedom of action, even our freedom of thought. I do not mean a 'Great Reset' such as our enemies have conceived, but at least a Great Reckoning to restore Justice and consequence for the innumerable Crimes Against Humanity unleashed against Mankind. When, like a mighty river Justice returns, the overlords will be destroyed as surely as Pharaoh and his chariots were destroyed when they chased Moses into the Red Sea (*Exodus* 14:26-28). I trust this book shall serve as armour and weapon in the battle ahead, for battle it is, and battle it will be.

Abdiel LeRoy

FROM THE AUTHOR

Thank you for reading this book, the third and final instalment in the *Battle Manuals for Freedom Series* (which you can find at https://Geni.us/Rights). If you have found value in it, I would value your review wherever you buy books. A few sentences would suffice.

If you think I've missed something important, or a link doesn't work, or you find some other glitch, let me know at RenewedTestament@protonmail.com. I am quick to make adjustments when readers point them out to me.

If you'd like updates from me, join my mailing list from my website, https://PoetProphet.com. I also post articles to Substack at *The Poet's Eye* (though I have been 'demonetized' there) and occasional videos to 'alternative' video-hosting sites such as Bastyon, BitChute, and Brighteon.

I don't bother with TikTok any more after it closed an account and savaged my remaining content with censorship, strikes, and shadow-bans, and I gave up on Facebook, YouTube, and Twitter long ago.

One way to support my work is to buy goldbacks with my affiliate link at https://Geni.us/Goldbacks. I earn a modest fee on any purchases you make there at no extra cost to you. You can also join the United Precious Metals Association at https://Geni.us/UPMA then transfer goldbacks to me using my email address, RenewedTestament@protonmail.com.

But the best way is to buy and review my books. My titles encompass fiction, non-fiction, memoir, poetry, and epic poetry, all listed below. You can avoid Amazon entirely now by buying direct at https://payhip.com/poetprophet.

When it comes to this series, I recommend the paperbacks if you're using them as battle manuals, then you can mark them up with notes, labels, and highlights for quick reference, but if you want to dig deeper, the eBooks will serve because they contain links to my online sources.

I don't offer individualized advice services, however. Sometimes, I hear from a reader, or someone who has watched one of my videos, setting out a lengthy description of their circumstances and asking what actions I suggest. I want to help, but my immediate calling is to write books, and I hope that shall suffice both to benefit you and to reward me. I also echo Tolkien's observation that "advice is a dangerous gift, even from the wise to the wise."

Finally, thank you for embracing this labour of love. May the Most High bless you and keep you, make his face to shine upon you, and give you everlasting life. May he go with you and ahead of you, a pillar of cloud by day and a pillar of fire by night, and bring you to places he hath prepared.

Abdiel LeRoy, 2024

EXTRAS

THE PARABLE OF THE FROGS

There once was a group of big, fat, greedy frogs, gathered around a puddle, and in that puddle were many thousands of tadpoles, but the water in that puddle was evaporating, so the tadpoles were confined into a smaller and smaller space and feared they might die before they could become frogs.

As I said, the frogs were very greedy, and they did not want to share the land with the tadpoles, so they sucked even more water from the puddle lest the tadpoles should survive to become frogs.

Some of the tadpoles looked up and saw the wicked plan of the frogs and tried to warn their fellows, but most were too frightened to listen. A few did get the message, though, which the frogs did not like at all. "What if these tadpoles united against us?" they said to one another. "Then some would surely survive and become frogs, and who knows what chaos would ensue?"

So they decided the best course of action would be to promise survival to some of the tadpoles if they would attack the troublemakers in the puddle and silence them by whatever means necessary. The frogs also trained their recruits in how to persuade others that the real source of their woes was not the frog overlords but other tadpoles, such as those with different markings, or who preferred different ways to live.

The frogs were very pleased with themselves when they saw the conflict this caused among the tadpoles, who formed into factions and attacked eachother, so that things became even more difficult in the puddle. Yet some tadpoles still looked up and saw the plan of the frogs and could not be persuaded to keep silent about it.

Then one day, those who looked up saw flying in the sky above a big white bird and, though they did not quite understand its significance yet, sensed there might be salvation in it. So they leapt from the water and splashed the surface, hoping the bird might see them. It took a few goes, but a ray of reflected light did eventually catch the eye of the bird, who looked down at the pitiful scene below.

"Well, that's odd!" the bird said to himself. "In our world, we guard our vulnerable, but these frogs appear to be doing the opposite to *their* kin."

With that, he swooped down from the clouds, and the frogs, who had been so focused on keeping the tadpoles down that they did not think to look up, had no idea of his approach until his shadow was upon them. Some tried to flee, but they were all so fat that none found the speed to get away. This way and that, the bird's murderous beak and razor-sharp talons tore into the flesh of the helpless frogs until not one was left alive!

And so, that day, the tadpoles were liberated. Fresh rains came that replenished their pool, and they could now grow freely into frogs. And as they remembered the oppression they had suffered, they did not repeat the cruelties of the first frogs, but allowed future generations of tadpoles to become themselves without fear or favour. And every year, in the season when frogs would become tadpoles, they all would sing a chorus of thanks to the great white bird who had saved them.

Of course, over time, tadpole and frog started to forget about the white bird, and it went from legend to myth to fairy tale, until most paid the story no heed at all or invented a religion around it that was really about worship of themselves. This emboldened later generations of frogs to repeat the wicked ways of their distant ancestors, who were not there to warn them of the danger.

But some vestige of the true memory remained, and whenever the frogs became wicked again, there would always be some tadpoles who would speak up and look up and call down help from the skies. And somehow, a ripple of light would catch the eye of a passing bird who would dispense his justice all over again.

Abdiel LeRoy

THE AWAKENING

Many were the souls that swept past me, their screams a vast orchestra of terror. They were flying, most of them, but there was no joy in their flight, only anguish and dread. I realized I too was mid-air, my soul also consumed with terror. And then…

That I was dead. We were all dead. Some terrible event had occurred to set us all adrift at once, dislocated spirits, suddenly removed from all we knew and loved, even our reassuring contact with the earth.

Yet, even in this state of limbo, untethered to hope, love, or connection, I began to sense that all was not lost, that we were not forever doomed to languish in agony of soul.

Some screamed still, but others, as I, began to settle and become quiet. We were waiting, and as the lamentations abated, they were replaced by a sound like rushing waters, accompanied by something like a warm breeze that brought comfort, as a golden glow began to permeate the gloom.

By now, all voices had ceased, and each of us became still, floating in air.

Then the glow brightened until it became almost too bright to behold. A flash of gold, and I found myself facing a great wingèd being so dazzling that I felt I would be consumed in his fire.

But when our eyes met, he immediately slipped into another state, his wings folded, and he became an outline in the whiteness, a moving sketch in ink, who seemed to sit before me. By now, all awareness of others was gone, and he and I sat face-to-face, as in private meeting.

But when he opened his mouth to speak, such a deafening roar came forth that once again I was put to terror. I motioned to scream myself, but no sound came forth.

Then the apparition, seeming almost as alarmed at the sound of his own voice as I, immediately put his hand to his mouth.

"Sorry about that," he said. "I'm new at this." His voice was gentle, deep, and reassuring.

Yet I was still too shocked to reply.

"Allow me to introduce myself," he continued. "I am Uriel. I stand in the presence of God."

At this, I took a deep breath as relief flooded my soul, and it was the first time since... since what shall I call it? My transmutation? My passage into another state of being?... that I even became aware that I had breath to breathe.

"I... I... I..."

"Yes, what you've experienced does tend to render mortals speechless at first, but I dare say you'll get the hang of it."

"You're Uriel?"

"Yes."

"I've heard of you. Aren't you Regent of the Sun? But you said you're new at this. So this is the first time you've..."

" 'Conveyed', we call it."

" 'Conveyed'? What does that mean?"

"Well, the battlefront's been a bit quiet of late. Not that the war in Heaven is any less intense, mind you. It's just that there's a lot more subtle stuff going on at the moment—intelligence-gathering, espionage, that sort of thing—so I thought I'd give conveyance a go. I've gone through all the training and made sure to fold my wings away when I approached you, become more human-like, and veil the fireglow. It's just my voice I forgot to change, and gave us *both* a fright. Again, please excuse."

"Um, I still don't know what 'conveyance' is."

"Ah yes, well, conveyance is when we come to souls newly released from their bodies..."

" 'Newly released from their bodies?' So I *am* dead."

"Hmm," said the angel, tilting his hand from side to side in a gesture of equivocation. "Your condition remains to be resolved, but in any case, you have nothing to fear."

"I see."

"No you don't, not really, but you will."

"So what happens now?"

"First, I need to introduce you to someone."

With that, I heard beautiful birdsong, followed by the sudden appearance of a little robin, russet of breast, tawny of tail and wings, who flew to some vaguely discernible perch between me and the angel.

Oh if I could describe his melody—so rich, so complex, so virtuous, but most of all, calming and reassuring. I had seen this little fellow often in my countryside walks in England and in its hedgerows and gardens, his presence always welcoming, always gladdening my heart. I had ever delighted in his song, but now I could discern its meaning, which I will try to set down here, however imperfectly.

"I am thy messenger, and always was,
Watched over you from Heaven and on Earth,
Prepared the way for you, from first to last,
And I was there to celebrate your birth."

Taking my lead from his manner of speech, I asked, "What is thy name?"

"You know my name," the bird replied, "for it is yours, honored and celebrated in your epic verse."

I gasped.

"I dared to hope it would be you
Who heard the prophet in a former age,
An age of wickedness, as is this one,
With new atrocity on History's page."

"Of such atrocity I come to speak,
An intercessor now divinely sent
To counter Mankind's fear and greed and hate.
All creatures of the Earth I represent.

"Soon shall my kind from tree branch disappear,
No longer shall our song herald God's call.
Birds, bees, and butterflies, from briar to brook,
Man will not stop 'til he has slaughtered all."

I knew his message to be true, the forces of destruction to be relentless and implacable, even slowing them down a superhuman challenge, let alone stopping them or repairing the devastation left in their rapacious wake.

"Heavy my heart to hear these dismal tidings,
That man's defilement of land, air, and sea,
Shall so persist as to extinguish hope,
Its dimming flame snuffed out eternally."

"But, man of God, this is not writ in stone.
If you and others like you overcome
The earthly powers now wielding their destruction,
The Will of God on Earth may yet be done."

"But it appears that I have left this Earth,"
I countered, "that my soul from body's split.
How then may I bring Heaven's Will to Earth
Without the vehicle to channel it?"

Now the robin turned to Uriel, who all this while had listened in silence to our conversation. The angel interjected:

"It's up to you now. I am come to give you three choices. In an instant, I could summon a chariot of fire to take you Heaven-ward and to the eternal realms. Or, with your namesake, you could fly the skies above the Earth and gladden receptive hearts. Or, your third choice, to return to Earth as your mortal self and enact the mission just described. In any case, you will be beloved and blessed of the Eternal Father, and your choice today can neither increase nor diminish that."

Uriel now nodded to the robin who, taking his cue, flew out of our circle, piping new melodies as he left. And once more, I was alone with the angel, to whom I thought aloud:

"Better it is to be with the Lord, to follow in Elijah's wake to Heaven immediately, or to take wing with the robin, but in either case, I'd leave behind such a scene of devastation. I love this Earth and all its beauty. And though a better place awaits, I cannot abandon it now. I must go back."

"Then be it so!" said the angel.

He immediately transformed, his eyes blazing like fire, a flash of gold again, then vanished in an instant. I found myself lying on a windswept heath, staring up at a pale sky. I touched my chest to verify that I was man and flesh again, a beating heart within. Shakily, I got to my feet, and saw that others were beginning to stir around me.

They were obviously bewildered, yet I detected in

their demeanour quiet resolve. I knew instinctively that they had just experienced a revelation similar to mine. In silence, we walked toward each other until we were a small group.

"For Heaven and Earth?" I asked.

"For Heaven and Earth," all replied.

And it was so.

Abdiel LeRoy

KING CHARLES' ADDRESS TO TROUBLESOME DISSENTERS

In the Year of Our Lord 2024, His Royal Highness King Charles III issued, by dint of his prerogative according to the Divine Right of Kings, the following Declaration...

To the subjects of our United Kingdom —

It has come to our attention that a growing number of you have appointed yourselves messengers of so-called truth in this day and age. You also contend that the time-honoured institutions of this nation—from pulpit to police station to Parliament—are somehow corrupted and not acting in your best interests.

Some of you have even become emboldened to criticize our Royal Personage and to allege all sorts of unpleasant acts committed by Our Person, such as killing off inconvenient wives, slaughtering children in Satanic rites, and then having the witnesses killed. The most villainous of you cite Article 61 of Magna Carta to argue our possessions, lands, and titles should be seized.

Vile creatures! Such hate-speech must, of course, be met with a strong and uncompromising response. Thus far, we have exercised great restraint, for we value the loyalty of our subjects and would not wish to invite public reproach, even for justifiable acts of moderate violence. Therefore, even with the many provocations and outrages against the dignity and reputation of Our Person, royal house, and government, we have conducted ourselves with generous indulgence of your follies.

True, our esteemed Metropolitan Police have tortured some of you, but this is entirely warranted during times of national emergency, whether that emergency be from viruses or war or climate change or what have you. It is no exaggeration to say—and we have done so on more than one occasion—that the challenges facing us today call for a military-style campaign on a global scale.

But now, we issue this Proclamation as a warning to the troublemakers among you, that our patience only goes so far, and that, for the sake of your own safety and for the Common Good, further transgressions against Our Person or against our noble ministers of State shall be met with harsher measures including, but not limited to, imprisonment with re-education, seizure of persons and possessions, administration of appropriate medical measures, and the removal of children from your families and from your seditious teachings. My dutiful ministers and Parliament have already written the laws to enact such responses as a final solution to your disobedient acts and words, and will not hesitate to use them as necessary.

Now, some of you may object to our use of the word 'laws' to describe our legislative Acts and decrees, but we do so in full acknowledgement of our sacred duty and authority as God's anointed representative on Earth. As he has delegated to Our Person his sole authority to write law, you should comply with our rules as if they were law, for they are really one and the same.

Charles ~~Saxe-Coburg~~ Windsor, Rex in Aeternum, &c.

KLAUS AND THE DEVIL

The old man wore his favourite garment for this much anticipated meeting, a long black robe with billowing sleeves and thick lapels that reflected the dim candlelight of the temple. Much blood had been spilled through the night onto the checkered tiles beneath his feet, for the cult devotees had done their job well. Since dusk, they had butchered long and hard with their sacrificial knives, while others watched, chanting and swaying in unison. And once the last drop of blood had been extracted, they practised upon each other astonishing feats of defilement.

These scenes were still playing in the mind of the man as he made his way across the alternating black and white tiles, but the temple was still again now. The floor had been hastily mopped, though the fetid odour of body fluids hung in the air. The altar itself had not been touched, and still steamed with the offal of sacrifice, dripping steadily onto the tiles beneath.

Would his shoes be stained? the man wondered. They were extremely rare and expensive, and he considered removing them before moving closer, but then he reasoned that, as they were a deep red colour to begin with, blood spatters wouldn't make much difference.

Behind the altar hung two braided curtains, fringed with gold, a slight gap between them, and a red glow pulsing from behind. The man trembled with anticipation.

"Klaus," said a drawling voice.

"Master," the man whispered back in fearful awe.

"Your work tonight was…"

"Master?"

"Satisfactory."

"Zank you, Master," said the man, though he had hoped for higher praise than this. "To bring you pleasure is our delight."

"And you did. And you did. Danke, Klaus," replied the voice.

"Bitte, Meister." He loved it when his lord addressed him in his native tongue.

"But now, we have other matters to discuss, do we not, Klaus?"

"As you wish, Master."

"Oh, be assured, I do wish. I wish very much."

"Yes, Master."

"So how's everything going with the Project, Klaus?"

"We are making good progress."

"Are you, Klaus? Are you really?"

There was something in the tone of this question that

unnerved the man. A chill passed down his body as he replied, "Yes, Master. Many have died."

"Hmm. What's your definition of 'many', Klaus?"

"Tens of millions."

"Oh dear, Klaus. 'Tens of millions,' you say. I'm afraid that won't do. There are still billions of humans running around the planet, yet you call that 'good progress.' I mean, yes you've managed to kill off some millions with the Weapon, and others have perished from famine, war, poison, and so on, but you're still woefully short of the target. Did I not instruct you to get the world's population down to 500 million? Did you not see the Georgia Guidestones before they were blown up?"

"Of course I am aware of zem, Master."

"Then you will also be aware that you are still several billion bodies short of the extermination target."

"We will do better, Master."

"Hmm."

"And ze Weapon hasn't reached its full effect yet."

"Ah yes, that brings me to another matter, Klaus, old boy. About the timing of that effect. Why did you kill off so many so quickly?"

"Master, was not extermination ze goal?"

"Yes, Klaus, extermination was *ze* goal."

Hearing this hint of mockery from his lord unnerved the man even more. For a moment, his cheek spasmed uncontrollably, until he managed to overcome his nerves.

"A for effort, Klaus," the voice continued, "but why did you kill and injure with such immediate effect? You see, with all these people keeling over just after the shot, and many of those caught on camera, you've alerted people to the danger."

"Zis was an oversight, my lord, but only because some of my colleagues were overzealous in zeir duty."

"Ha! Overzealous, you call it? Downright reckless, I'd say. You were supposed to install gradual decay into their bodies so that we might have plausible deniability, but now, with all these videos circulating of athletes and news anchors dropping like flies, people falling under trains and what have you, you have badly tipped our hand. What an appalling lack of discipline..."

"Master, I will put it right..."

"I haven't finished. Not only did you alert people to the danger prematurely, you robbed us of our pleasure in the slow torture of our Enemy's beloved creatures."

"Forgive me, Master."

"Forgive you? What do you take me for, Klaus, to suppose forgiveness is in *my* nature?"

The man had no answer, and his cheek spasmed again, and this time it took him longer to bring it back under control.

"And another question," the voice went on. "Why did you roll out the Weapon at the beginning of 2021? You made it stupidly easy for them to chart excess deaths on a year-by-year basis. Why didn't you introduce it mid-way through the year so that you could fudge the numbers better?

"We will do better with ze next pandemic."

"*Ze* next pandemic, eh? Perhaps, perhaps."

"Yes, we have ze next variant ready to go."

"Oh Klaus, now you're starting to bore me. That narrative has been going rapidly downhill since, what was it, Omicron? And then what came after, Ninja or some such? And then you got really sexy with, what, BA1 and BA2? Listen, Klaus, old fellow. How are people going to be fearful of some new variant if they can't even remember its name? Even I can't keep them all straight!"

"I understand, Master, but next we shall bring a new disease: Marburg, perhaps, or Ebola."

"They're hardly new, though, are they, Klaus?"

"But we have changed zem in ze laboratory."

"Ah! Have you now? More spike protein, perhaps? More snake venom? The problem is you have made people so distrustful after your premature kill spree that you've made it ever so much harder to mount another fear campaign. What is it those disgusting humans say? 'Fool me once…' and all of that? No, Klaus, on due reflection, I'm going to have to rethink my strategy. You and the World Economic Forum are really not fit for purpose."

A gasp of disbelief escaped from the old man's mouth, and even his best efforts could not keep his cheek spasms in check. "But, Master," he pleaded, "we did our best."

"Oh Klaus, you do amuse me. Did your best? You're starting to sound like a Christian. Our Enemy may be disposed to bestow his 'unmerited favour' on those who love him, in spite of their many failures, but surely you don't think *I'm* going to do that, do you? No, I'm going to get rid of the WEF and, for that matter, the United Nations and the World Health Organization. And I'm going to destroy them all by the hand of my real agent on Earth."

"But, my lord, am I not your agent?"

"Oh Klaus, don't be absurd. Your cover is blown, you're a laughing stock. No-one will believe you. No, the one I have appointed will appear as a saviour by going after the likes of you, but in the end will turn out to be an even worse tyrant than those he removes. Devilishly clever, don't you think, even if I do say so myself? Yes, we'll start with a soft kill at first, but it won't be long before he goes full Man-of-Lawlessness, if you get my drift. He will break you and your little Davos club, for so it is written. Nothing personal, you understand."

"But Master, all my years of service."

"Yes, I know. It's most unfortunate. All your years of service will, I fear, earn you more punishment at the hands of the Enemy. But do go on, Klaus. You're really quite entertaining."

"You promised me a reward!"

By now, the man had lost some of his fear as it gave way to deep-seated anger, resentment, and betrayal.

"Oh, that?" said the voice. "You mean you want me to extend your life? Not in my toolbox, old boy. Did you not drink enough adrenochrome then, Klaus?"

"Yes, but..."

"Did you not drink enough children? You and your chums got through quite a few tonight."

"Yes, but..."

"Ah, you mean... What was it you said in one of your boring little speeches? 'Fusion of our physical, digital, and biological identities.' Is that what you mean? You want your consciousness to be put in a chip and then keep yourself going in a machine or a skin or some such?"

"Not exactly, Master. You promised..."

"Stop right there, Klaussy Boy. I promised, did I? You do know what the Scriptures call me, don't you?"

"Yes, Master. You are called Lucifer."

"Well, yes, that's one name, but you seem to be forgetting something, Klaus, old boy."

"I don't follow, Master."

"Oh but I think you do, Klaus. Come on, you can do it. What else do they call me?"

"Ze Morning Star."

"Good. Keep going."

"Prince of ze Air, and ze Accuser."

"Bravo, Klaus, but you're still missing the key term here, old chap.

"You prowl like a lion."

"Yes, yes, yes, all of that, but you're still not hitting the mark there, Klaussy Boy, are you? Shall I spell it out for you? Shall I be plain? They call me Father of Lies, do they not?"

"Yes, Master."

"And do you suppose the Father of Lies makes promises and then keeps them? Who do you think I am? Our Enemy? Again, Klaus, you're sounding alarmingly like a Christian."

"Please, Master. Give me anozer chance. I shall bring more war, more deception, more famine, and we shall reach our target by 2030. We shall have more bioweapons, energy weapons, poison ze water, ze air, ze food, more radiation, more censorship, more surveillance, more legislation, cyber attacks, quarantine camps, more taxes and fines and fees to break ze will of ze people, und so on."

"Oh, Klaus, aren't you adorable? Bargaining with me to procure what? Mercy? I don't do mercy, Klaus. You should know that by now. 'The quality of mercy is not strained. It droppeth as the gentle rain from Heaven upon the place beneath.' Blah Blah Blah. Das ist Qwatsch, Klaus!"

The man's knees were shaking now, whether from fear or anger, an effect heightened by his interrogator's return to his native language, not to praise this time but in rebuke.

"Of course, I'm not into rain, either," the voice continued, "not normal rain, I mean. I go in more for tornadoes, hurricanes, earthquakes, floods, forest fires, you know the type of thing, what they foolishly call 'natural' disasters."

"Please, Master, I beg you..."

"Ah, that's more like it, Klaus, begging me, acknowledging my power over you, but it's still too late, old boy. You see, I've grown weary of you. Now run along and tell Justin to come in. He's waiting outside. I'm in need of some stimulation of a more physical nature, and he always proves most willing to oblige."

"Master, I could perform zis function if you wish."

"Oh, Klaus. The very thought. How revolting. Do I seem that desperate to you?"

"Zat's not what I mean. I mean I can do... ze special zings."

"Oh where have I heard that before? Let me think. Emmanuel said it, Rishi said it, Tony said it, Boris said it, Jacinda said it, and so did Chrystia, Ursula, and even horrid little Theresa. And yet every single one of them profoundly disappointing, I do assure you. Quite without personality, wholly without charm. And, come to think of it, since they're all your little acolytes, Klaus, I really thought you would have trained them better.

"Now, don't get me wrong. It's not that I'm especially fond of Justin. The boy is an absolute dullard, and even dimmer of intellect than all the rest of you, but he is at least accommodating, and that shall suffice for now. Come to think of it, Klaus, do you know who else was in here just the other day offering me 'special zings,' as you put it?"

"I don't know," the man replied wearily.

"Your mate, Charlie boy Windsor! Well, of course, I was so disgusted by the very *idea* of old Sausage Fingers coming anywhere near me that I was tempted to put him out of his misery right there and then. But alas, I'm not permitted to until the Enemy tells me it's time, and apparently, his crimes must be revealed first. Which won't be long now, of course. The Kamloops and Caernarvon revelations are well underway."

"Master, I could bring more evidence against him."

"Down to your last straw now, are you, Klaus? Throwing your friends under the bus to buy yourself a little more time? No, Klaus, there's no need. His fate is sealed... as is yours. Now then, entertaining as this discourse has been, I have other matters to attend to. I'm sure you can understand the burdens of running a global empire. Permit me to dispense with the customary pleasantries such as 'Goodbye' or 'Farewell', much less 'God bless you'. In your case, none of them applies."

"Master! Master!" the man called desperately, but it was all in vain. The red light behind the curtain dimmed to an almost imperceptible glow, and Klaus knew in an instant that all his life's work was for naught. Soon, he would join his mentor Henry in permanent exile from life.

Perhaps that had been the plan all along, to use him and then to discard him as so much medical waste. He would be dead within the day, he was sure of that.

Barely able to stay on his feet, the man shuffled his way back across the checkered tiles and out into the hallway. There, sitting anxiously on a chair beside the wall, was little Justin, ever eager to please. He rose to greet his tutor and extended his hand.

"Hello Klaus," he said with his ingratiating smile. "Good to see you again."

Klaus did not return the gesture, didn't even turn his head to look at the supplicant awaiting his turn to enter the chamber. "Fuck off, you little shit!" he replied, and marched resolutely towards the front door.

Two security men followed him to the vestibule, but Klaus dismissed them with an impatient flick of his hand. Not even an army could protect him now. He put on his coat, eager to cover the expensive robe which now seemed so preposterous, even to his own eyes.

Off came the red shoes too. He didn't even bother undoing the laces this time but held down the back of each shoe with the front of his other foot and hurriedly peeled them off. Cursing under his breath, he picked up his normal shoes from a shoe rack before him and slipped them on. His hands were trembling too much to tie the laces so he left them loose.

He made his way out of the front door and staggered down the front steps of the lodge. The air was cold, and a dim light ahead signalled the beginning of a new day, the close of which he did not expect to see. He took a few deep breaths of the chilly morning air and felt a giddy delight as condensation formed from his breath. These may be his final moments, but at least he would enjoy this last palpable token of life.

His path led him past a garbage bin, where he tossed the red shoes, then towards an old church on his right. It had a sad, dilapidated look to it now. There had been many more funerals there of late, but fewer weddings, and hardly any christenings. Its life was hanging by a thread. He had achieved that much at least, the man thought to himself. Should he go in there now and confess his sins? He laughed at the idea. "Too late for zat now, Klaussy Boy," he chuckled to himself, recalling snippets of the chilling conversation he had just had in the temple lodge.

On the next block, he walked past a school playground where, soon enough, the din of playful children would be heard. "We didn't kill enough of you," he whispered to himself.

Immediately, his mind began weaving the old equations, how a rising death count would promote him in the eyes of his collaborators in the secret society, and how the youngest victims would count the most because they were closest to the God he hated. The ones who survived would be trained and traumatized to become wholly indifferent to the suffering of others, a generation of cold-blooded killers, ready to follow orders without question and complete the work of annihilation.

Klaus stopped, placing his hands on the chain-link fence outside the playground, looked in, and sighed. At that moment, a ray of sunlight kissed the side of his face.

"You know this will be the last time you feel the sun, don't you?" said a voice on his left.

Klaus turned to see who had spoken. A man was standing beside him, wearing a white robe that shimmered in the morning breeze. He too was looking into the playground, but his eyes shone as white fire.

It was time.

January 2024

BOOKS BY A. LEROY (ABDIEL LEROY)

NON-FICTION

KNOW YOUR MEDICAL RIGHTS

Did you know that, under international law, no-one can demand you get a medical test, wear a mask, or have any other medical procedure?

And did you also know that no emergency, even if it threatens the life of a nation, takes away any of your rights? Or that any politician or pundit who attempts to persecute a group based on medical status is committing a Crime Against Humanity?!

Meanwhile, international law also confirms YOUR MEDICAL STATUS IS CONFIDENTIAL, a protection supported by medical codes dating back millennia to the Hippocratic Oath.

Yet governments are not only demanding we hand over this sacred information but are still using it to divide and discriminate, penalizing bodily sovereignty and autonomy, and they are poised to inflict even worse atrocities than they did during 'COVID'.

"I know in my heart that these measures are an atrocity," writes Abdiel LeRoy in the Introduction, "and my spirit rebels against them, but just having that instinct is not enough now. WHAT ARE MY RIGHTS?"

Here is your constitutional Bible, a rebuking voice to tyranny, and a rallying cry for all Mankind.

KNOW YOUR LAWFUL RIGHTS

Not since the days of Noah has Earth witnessed such an all-out assault on life and livelihood as we see today. The false authorities are pursuing their agenda of extermination and enslavement with a ruthlessness most of us could never have imagined.

In this sequel to *Know Your Medical Rights*, Abdiel LeRoy dismantles the lies, programming, and conditioning that have kept us from ourselves. He reminds you who you are, a three-dimensional being standing above the two-dimensional fictions of government, and he empowers you to tear down strongholds of dogma and dictatorship.

"I will show you that all is counterfeit, all theatre," LeRoy writes in the Introduction, "and that counterfeit governments, issuing counterfeit currencies and writing counterfeit legislation masquerading as Law, are wielding counterfeit authority. It's so much easier to refuse and refute that authority when you know its enforcers are beneath you and that they are peddling fictional constructs."

Then, having pierced through the illusions and mind-tricks of tyrants, he lays before you the weapons of True Law you will need to regain your Sovereignty and Birthright. This book will serve you as armour and weapon in the battles ahead.

KNOW YOUR FINANCIAL RIGHTS

Your tax compliance has been funding genocide. Your debt payments are rewarding banks who never lent you anything in the first place. Meanwhile, any digits in your bank account can be seized or freezed at a moment's notice.

The entire financial system has been engineered to extort us, enslave us, and then finally to exterminate us when we've nothing left to give. It's time to tear it down and stop funding our demise, and it's time to transact in ways that tyrants can not monitor, surveil, and control.

Know Your Financial Rights is the final installment of a tyrant-slaying trilogy of constitutional bibles, recalling the mission of Bible prophets who overthrew kings.

Wear this book as a garment of protection, wield it as a spiritual sword, and weaponize it against the legion of traitors now conspiring against us.

THE GOURMET GOSPEL COLLECTION

A Better Eden/ It Was for Freedom/ Foes to Grace

Desperate to escape from an eating disorder, Abdiel went on a quest for "the truth that sets me free," and found it in a rediscovery of Grace—the unmerited favor of God—that church teachings rarely, if ever, reveal.

With the help of great writers, Christian thinkers, and of course the Bible itself, he returns to an Eden of the mind that predates the command, 'Do not…', and where sin is neither possible nor perceived.

DUELING THE DRAGON COLLECTION

Five Memoirs About Living and Working in China

A wide-eyed expat is detained by Beijing cops and told to sign a false confession. Will he make it out of China alive? *Dueling the Dragon* is a great adventure story, but *this* one just happens to be true!

With a journalist's eye and lively wit, LeRoy's memoirs expose the deep levels of corruption tearing at China's social fabric.

MY PORTABLE PARADISE

Transform Your Life Through House Sitting

Tired of burning bitter hours in a toxic job? Tired of the same old routine? Tired of the stress and hassle of paying rent, or a mortgage? Then house sitting may be for you.

From a beach house in Costa Rica, this veteran house sitter and author welcomes you to share in the joys and blessings he has received.

Whether you're a 'digital nomad' looking for adventure, retired and seeking a change of scenery, or just looking for a simpler life, you'll find gentle guidance in this book. And… it might just change your life!

POETRY COLLECTIONS

WELL VERSED

To Shakespeare, Poets, and the Performing Arts

Dante is famous. He imagined Hell,
A plain of burning flakes and sulphurous smell,
Pour souls afflicted in a sorry state,
And names the enemies he loves to hate.

But he's no match for Milton's inspiration,
No poet greater in imagination.
Yet Shakespeare most gets ink within these pages.
'Twas he who said, "Our praises are our wages!"

VERSES VERSUS EMPIRE

I—The Bush Era

It's Judgment Day, and George W. Bush strides confidently towards the throne of God. How will the Almighty respond? Find out in this work of devastating satire.

From Bush through Obama to Trump, LeRoy charts an epic course through the inferno of U.S. politics, exposing the fraud and folly of empire and its rulers.

VERSES VERSUS EMPIRE

II—The Obama Era

As the late historian Howard Zinn said, "There have only been a handful of people who use their wit to take down the pretensions of the high and mighty."

Here is one of them, a resounding voice for our times, an offering of hope and beauty rising from the ashes of a broken political system, a creation of unprecedented literary power. Witness herein that the pen really *is* mightier than the sword!

VERSES VERSUS EMPIRE

III—The Trump Era

The intellectuals of this dangerous age,
However eloquent, however sage,
Indicting empire with insightful prose,
Have not yet healed the nation's woes.

To tear down strongholds of the powers-that-be
Who give lip service to Democracy,
A poet of prophetic voice steps forward
To prove the pen is mightier than the sword!

THE VERSES VERSUS EMPIRE COLLECTION

Poetry and Prose on Three Imperial Presidencies

2001-2021

Through three imperial presidencies
The poet cries, voice in the wilderness,
Reed swaying in the wind,[i] *a bruisèd reed,*[ii]
His motion stirred to music,
Daring to see and state the obvious,
Decry hypocrisy, prophetically to see
Not just the future but the now,
The awful now and make some sense of it,
The world a stage on which plays out
Congressional pantomime, a knot
Unable to untie itself. The blood
Of innocents cries out to Heaven where
These incensed lines as incense burn
With hate of Hate and hope of Hope.

---

i. Matthew 11:7.
ii. Matthew 12:20.

EPIC POETRY

(FICTION IN VERSE)

ELIJAH

A Fictional Reinvention of the Great Prophet's Life in an Epic Poem

He called down fire and false prophets slew,
He raised the dead, conversed with angels, flew
To Heaven in a chariot of fire
And fled from Jezebel's murderous ire.

But there is more, O so much more to tell,
Of meeting Moses and a dragon's spell,
Shapeshifting goddesses at Cherith Brook.
Such wonders will unfold within this book!

OBAMA'S DREAM

The Journey That Changed the World

This sordid theatre we call politics
Is full of lies and dirty tricks,
But what if angels came into the fray
To challenge presidents and what they say?

And what if one appeared before God's throne
Where wicked schemes of men are overthrown
And Satan tried a victim to condemn?
This book turns upside-down the world of men!

THE EPICS COLLECTION

Obama's Dream, Elijah, Jezebel's Lament

It is an age-old struggle, that between
The earthly power of presidents and kings
Encountering divine power, wonders seen
When prophets pray. This theme the author brings

In reinvention of the Bible tales,
Ascents to Heaven, wondrous revelation,
Shapeshifting goddesses in his portrayals,
Joined by the author's audiobook narrations.

FICTION

JEZEBEL'S LAMENT

A Defense of Reputation, a Denouncement of the prophets Elijah and Elisha

In this companion piece to *Elijah*, Israel's tyrant queen tells her side of the story and why she so detests that "unkempt fire-and-brimstone hairy hermit" who prophesies dogs shall eat her corpse.

"Yes, I had to get rid of some inconvenient men of God along the way, and a stubborn wine producer, but in all this I did only what a queen *must* do in such circumstances to protect herself, to safeguard her family and the royal line."

You will hear of trysts and treason in this witty rendering by Abdiel LeRoy.

THE CHRISTMAS TREE

A Tale of Divine Awakening

A tree is torn from his forest home and all that he loves, but there is courage in the heart of a little boy to protect his belovèd tree.

The author dreamt up this story from witnessing Christmas trees being abandoned on city sidewalks, but here his invention of a magical journey for one such tree will transport you through time and space and otherworldly encounter, even to the throne of God!

THE PRINCE'S OATH

A Tale From Afghanistan

An innocent man must lose his freedom, an innocent girl must yield her virginity, in this traditional tale from an era of kings.

From bandit attacks in a forest to treacherous plots at court, love will undergo many trials with the Almighty's help, even if it comes in the form of a cheeky little mouse!

THE CHRISTIAN REVERIES COLLECTION

The Christmas Tree/ The Prince's Oath/ Obama's Dream

You'll know a tree according to its fruit,
Three golden branches with one holy root,
The Good Book's inspiration running through,
This trinity uplifting hearts anew.

Not 'R'-rated as the Epics Collection,
These tales are more of a 'PG' selection,
But still have magic, shapeshifters, and all
Those elements mythology recalls.

APPENDIX

QUOTES FROM UPTON SINCLAIR'S 'THE JUNGLE' (1906)

I am an avid collector of quotes, and could fill many books just with those I have gathered, copied, typed out, or transcribed over decades. As I was preparing this book, my eye ran across my Upton Sinclair collection from *The Jungle* (1906). These speak so powerfully to our times that I list some here in this appendix.

> "He learned that America differed from Russia in that its government existed under the form of a democracy. The officials who ruled it, and got all the graft, had to be elected first, and so there were two rival sets of grafters, known as political parties, and the one which bought the most votes got the office."

> "Who can figure the cost of war to humanity—not merely the value of the lives and the material that it destroys, not merely the cost of keeping millions of men

in idleness, of arming and equipping them for battle and parade—but the drain upon the vital energies of society by the war attitude and the war terror."

"And then the subject became Religion. Government oppressed the body of the wage slave, but Religion oppressed his mind, and poisoned the stream of progress at its source. The workingman was to fix his hopes upon a future life, while his pockets were picked in this one."

"There are a million people, men and women and children, who share the curse of the wage slave, who toil every hour they can stand and see, for just enough to keep them alive, who are condemned till the end of their days to monotony and weariness, to hunger and misery, to heat and cold, to dirt and disease, to ignorance and drunkenness and vice!

"And then turn over the page with me, and gaze upon the other side of the picture. There are a thousand —ten thousand, maybe—who are the masters of these slaves, who own their toil... Their life is a contest among themselves for supremacy in ostentation and recklessness, in the destroying of useful and necessary things, in the wasting of the labor and the lives of their fellow creatures, the toil and anguish of the nations, the sweat and tears and blood of the human race! It is all theirs—it comes to them, just as all the springs pour into streamlets, and the streamlets into rivers, and the rivers into the oceans—so, automatically and inevitably, all the wealth of society comes to them.

"The farmer tills the soil, the miner digs in the earth, the weaver tends the loom, the mason carves the stone, the clever man invents, the shrewd man directs, the wise man studies, the inspired man sings—and all the result, the products of the labor of brain and muscle, are gathered into one stupendous stream and poured into their laps!"

www.ingramcontent.com/pod-product-compliance
Lightning Source LLC
LaVergne TN
LVHW052310200926
848481LV00002B/521
* 9 7 8 1 9 1 7 0 7 3 9 5 0 *